LOOKING AT A FAR MOUNTAIN

'Un oeil qui regarde bien, la voix qui vit'
An eye that sees, the voice that lives.

Edmond Rostand
1868–1918

From Cyrano de Bergerac

LOOKING AT A FAR MOUNTAIN

A STUDY OF KENDO KATA

Paul Budden

TUTTLE PUBLISHING
Boston • Rutland, Vermont • Tokyo

First Tuttle edition in 2000, an imprint of Periplus Editions (HK) Ltd,
with editorial offices at 153 Milk Street, Boston, Massachusetts 02109.

Library of Congress Catalog Card Number: Cataloging in Progress
ISBN: 0-8048-3245-5

Distributed by

NORTH AMERICA
Tuttle Publishing
Distribution Center
Airport Industrial Park
364 Innovation Drive
North Clarendon, VT
05759-9436
Tel: (802) 773-8930
Tel: (800) 526-2778
Fax: (802) 773-6993

JAPAN
Tuttle Publishing
RK Building, 2nd Floor
2-13-10 Shimo-Meguro,
Meguro-Ku
Tokyo 153 0064
Tel: (03) 5437-0171
Fax: (03) 5437-0755

ASIA PACIFIC
Berkeley Books Pte Ltd
5 Little Road #08-01
Singapore 536983
Tel: (65) 280-1330
Fax: (65) 280-6290

1 3 5 7 9 10 8 6 4 2
06 05 04 03 02 01 00

Printed in United States of America
Cover design by Jill A. Feron

CONTENTS

ACKNOWLEDGEMENTS

I would like to thank a number of people who have assisted in the bringing about of this study, either with background information and technical expertise, or by just supporting the venture and for putting up and practising with me over the past years.

Special thanks to:

Hideko and Les Denniston

Shoji Enomoto, Associate Professor in Faculty of Art and Letters, Nanzan University, Nagoya, Japan

Victor Harris, Curator Japanese Antiquities, British Museum

Kenji Hirose, Hanshi, Kodokan Kendo Dojo, Kyoto, Japan

Nobuo Hirakawa, Professor Meiji University, Tokyo, Japan

Terry Holt

Masayoshi Imasato, Associate Professor, Kendo Dept. Kyoto Sangyo University, Japan

Takeshi Kudoh, Kyoshi 7th Dan, All Japan Kendo Federation

Brian Kay, Director Eikoku News Digest, London

Jumpei Matsumoto, friend and fellow student in Kendo

Torao Ono, Kyoshi, Seijudo Kendo Dojo, Setagaya, Japan

Hiroyuki Shioiri, Associate Professor, Saitama University, Japan

Masatake Sumi, Professor, Dept. of Health and Physical Education, Fukuoka University of Education, Japan

Dr Haru-Hisa Takamatsu DVM.MS Ph.D

Peter Wells

To Yoshinori Inoue, fellow practitioner of the Kata, Tsuyako Suzuki for all her patience and kindness and to Goro Ohtaki, life long student of Musashi and without whose guidance and friendship this project would never have been attempted.

'Humility is indeed endless.'

Finally to my wife Helen, for her tolerance and understanding throughout.

Photos in the technical section by Malcom Birkitt.

Books used in reference and photographic reproduction courtesy of Shoji Enomoto.

Jikishin kage Ryu No Kata by Meishin Saito 1901 (Meiji 34)

Budo Hokan-Showa Tenran Shiai Huroku Dai Nihon Yuben Kai 1930 (showa 5)

Shinsei Kendo Kyokasho by Goro Saimura and Kinji Kaneko 1931 (showa 6)

Kai Tei Teikoku Kendo Kyohan by Kinnosuke Ogawa 1937 (showa 12)

Other photos courtesy of Kodansha Ltd., Tokyo, Japan

Pictures of Sasamori sensei via Victor Harris

Front Kanji (Japanese Lettering) by Kenji Hirose

Inside Kanji for Technical section by Tsuyako Suzuki

Note on the origins of the calligraphy illustrating this book:

Kenji Hirose sensei was born in Kyoto in 1905, and joined Kodokan dojo in 1924. His teacher was Kinnoske Ogawa who was not only the founder of Kodokan, but was recognised as one of the greatest kendo teachers of his age. Hirose sensei was a diligent student and studied with sincerity under Ogawa sensei until his teacher's death in 1962. Throughout his kendo career he won countless national and local competitions, and now at the age of 85 is still an active member of the same dojo he joined 66 years ago, teaching children and adults alike. He is 7th. dan Hanshi, and one of the most respected kendo teachers in Japan.

PREFACE

As a Kendo friend of the author, Mr. Paul Budden, since our first meeting in 1983, on occasion of the Kendo Summer Camp organized by the All Japan Kendo Federation for kendoists abroad, I am very happy to be granted a chance to write some comments in order to celebrate his book on *Kendo-kata*.

I am convinced that readers will find many important things, not only technical clues for practising *Kata* correctly, but also the historical facts which will be of great help to understand how the essence of *Kata* was established into ten forms as it is now.

We Japanese are taught to follow three steps when learning *Budo*, (martial ways), *Sado* (tea ceremony), *Kado* (flower arrangement) or any kind of traditional arts. It is 守 (*shu*, obeissance to *Kata* or what is taught by Sensei), 破 (*ha*, literally the destruction of it, but we may safely say it is the stage of individualization or digestion of *Kata* or what is taught) and 離 (*ri*, separation from it but always on the correct way without thinking or trying to be so).

The first step for us to master Kendo is to learn and practice *Kihon* (the fundamentals); *Suburi* (swing with a *Shinai*). *Ashisabaki* (footwork), *Kamae* (postures), and *Tenouchi* (grip of a *Shinai*). To repeat *Kihon* is an attempt, in other words, to put oneself into a *Kata* following in perfect obedience to one's Sensei. You may find it uncomfortable and constrained to follow the *Kata* at first, but once you master it, you will get to know the fact that to be in *Kata* is very comfortable, and that the *Kata* is not in the least restrictive but even very creative.

I sincerely hope that readers of this book will practice *Kata* repeatedly until you can find by experience that *Kata* is very profitable for your Kendo both mentally and technically.

Associate Professor of Saitama University
International Committee Member of
All Japan Kendo Federation,

Hiroyuki SHIOIRI

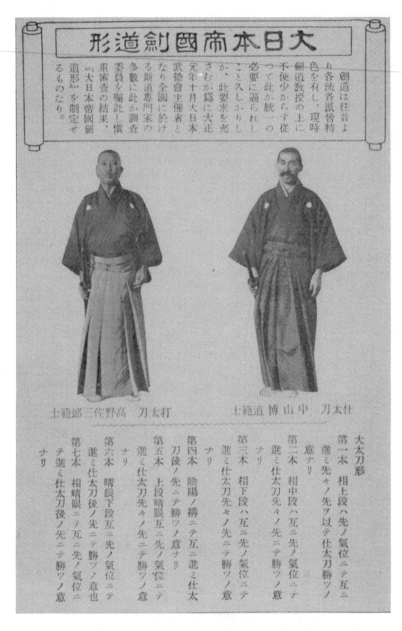

INTRODUCTION

This study has several aims, the most important being to offer some small insight (so vast is the subject) into the history, background and formulation of *nihon kendo kata*, thus forming a testimonial to the greatness of the masters who conceived the wonderful standardisation originally known as *Dai nihon Teikoku Kendo Kata*. Such is their importance to *Kendo* that I had hoped to be able to link up the individual forms of *dai nihon teikoku kata* to their original influences. Unfortunately, this has proved to be virtually impossible, although the genealogical reference diagram does indicate the masters of the various committees involved, and it is possible from this to determine the influences and origins of *Kendo* and the *Kata*. Indeed, the foremost influence is to be found within the *kodachi* forms where there is a strong resemblance to *Itto ryu Kodachi Kata*.

The modern *Nihon Kendo Kata* should be practised and studied with great reverence and respect, partly because of the important tradition and partly as an acknowledgement of the many schools and styles associated with those great men.

'By practising now in the present, we pay homage to the past and safeguard its continuation for the future'.

Perhaps this is the only justification necessary for *Kendo*, whose essence and entity is the true ethic of swordsmanship.

In reference to the *Nihon Kendo Kata* as practised today, the *Kata* was performed by myself and Mr. Yoshinori Inoue, both of us *Yondan* (4th Degree). This was done with the intention of establishing some reference points in order to facilitate the study of the *Kata*. Neither of us confess to being experts in *Kata* but tried only to perform to the best of our ability and limited understanding.

It may be necessary throughout the book to refer to the Glossary of Terms.

Teikoku *Kendo Kata-Kinnosuke Ogawa* on the right,
Shigesaburo Miyazaki on the left.

Picture taken in front of the grave of Ono Tadaaki, founder of the *Ono Ha Itto Ryu*,
successor to Ito Ittosai. *Junzo Sasamori* – right; Naritomo Tsurumi on the left.
They are performing *Ono Ha Itto Ryu kata*.

CHAPTER ONE

THE *KATA* TRADITION

In the pre *Tokuga* era, *Kata* were referred to as *kumitachi* and *seiho* and were the result of the training methods of the classical schools of *kenjutsu*. However, these methods did not actually become laid down and recorded officially until the period 1560–1572. They were developed from actual fighting techniques as taught by military teachers skilled in their art, and former techniques of classical swordsmanship contain the theory and practical applications necessary to retain the essence of their conception, and are thus vital for further development in all *kendoka*. In 1886 *Meiji* (19) the Japanese Police were the first, other than the existing classical schools, to refer to these old forms in order to create a standard *kendo kata*. In the same year the *keishichoryu kata* became the standard *kata* for police use, formed from the schools of *Jikishinkage, Kurama, Tsutsumi, Hozan, Risshin, Hokushin Itto, Asayama Ichiden, Jigen, Shinto Munen, Yagyu* and *Kyoshin Meichi Ryus*. It is interesting that the Japanese Police still use the *kata* system today as a highly beneficial training method, so maintaining the direct link to the origins of classical swordsmanship.

In 1895 *Meiji* (28) the foundation of the *Dai Nihon Butokukai* became the controlling body of all *budoka* throughout Japan, offering unity and attempting to standardise the classical *ryuha* or schools and sections.

This unification only really began after the war against Russia in 1904, 1905 (*Meiji* 37 and 38), through the foundation of the *Bujutsu Kyoin Yoseijo* (martial arts masters training school), in *Kyoto*, as research developed new *kata* in both *Judo* and *Kendo*.

In 1906, *Meiji* (39), *Noboru Watanbe* was the head of the *Dai Nihon Butokukai* committee, *Hanshi, Shinto Munen Ryu* together with *Unpachiro Shibae (Hanshi Shinto Munen Ryu), Kanichiro Mitsuhashi (Musashi ryu), Sekishiro Tokuno (hanshi, Jikishin kage ryu), Daisaku Sakabe (hanshi, kyoushin meichi ryu), Shingoro Negishi (Hanshi, Shinto munen ryu), Morie Abe (Jikishin kage ryu)*, and eight others who were allowed to take part in the discussions: were *T Naito, S Sayama, M Toyama, K Yano, K Minatobe, T Yamasato* and *H Nakayama*. In August 1906 the original three *kata* were decided as the *Butokukai Kenjutsu Kata*, also known as *Ten, Chi, Jin no Kata* Heaven, earth and person, or *jodan gedan chudan*. However, it seems that as very little discussion actually took place there was widespread complaint from the masters, making it unpopular and consequently little is known about this *Kata*.

In this same period the other leading group was the *Tokyo Koto Shihan Gakko*, or the teachers training college in Tokyo, with the founder of modern *judo, Jigoro Kano*, as its headmaster. *Tokyo Koto Shihan Gakko* organised a seminar and published the original *kata* of three forms, originated in 1911 by *Sasaburo Takano, I Ozawa, S Hoshino, A Tanaka, T Naito, S Negishi, T Shingai, H Nakayama, T Yamasato, S Kobayashi, S Kimura, K Shibata* and *Shigeyoshi Takano*.

Upon reading the original documents it is clear that there is a strong resemblance between these three forms of the *Tokyo Koto Shihan Gakko* and the first three forms of the *Dai Nihon Teikoku kendo kata*. Therefore it can be stated that the first three forms of *Dai Nihon Teikoku Kendo kata* had probably been formulated before the committee of *Butokukai* or their *kata* was established, or the official *Dai Nihon Teikoku kendo kata* of 1912 was published. In December 1911 (*Meiji* 44) the *Butokukai* formed a second committee with *Sasaburo Takano* (from *Koto Shihan Gakko*), *Takaharu Naito* (*Dai Nihon Butokukai*), *Tadashi Monna* (*Dai Nihon Butokukai*), *Shingoro Negishi* from (*Shinto Munen ryu*), *Shinpei Tsuji* from (*Saga*) and 20 other members. From this committee there appeared in November 1912 (*Taisho* 1) the publication of the *Dai Nihon Teikoku kendo kata* followed by a teaching seminar.

Translation of the Original Edict

Dai Nihon Teikoku Kendo Kata

The *kendo* schools suffer from a lack of unity, and we the *Dai Nihon Butokukai* have experienced many difficulties in teaching *kendo*, and although we feel these schools should keep their various characteristics, we have felt the necessity for unity through a standardisation programme, so in October of 1912 we entrusted research into various schools of swordsmanship, by several *kendo* masters. As the result of our careful study, we now establish the *Dai Nihon Teikoku kendo kata*.

It is important to note that not only did *Sasaburo Takano* (1862–1950) contribute greatly to the *Dai Nihon Teikoku Kendo Kata*, but that he is directly responsible for the formalisation of the *Gogyo No Kata* forms. His grandfather was *M. Takano*, headmaster of the *Ono ha Itto ryu*. *Sasaburo Takano* studied and practised fluently in this style as well as teaching modern *kendo* methods and from the essence of *Ono Ha Itto ryu kata* he developed the *Gogyo No Kata* and taught it to the students of the Tokyo *koto shihan gakko*. This college was the predecessor of the Tokyo University of Education which in turn was the predecessor of the present *Tsukuba* University where the *Gogyo No Kata* is still taught in its original forms, as well as at other selected universities.

In September 1917 (*Taisho* 6) the annotation of the *Dai Nihon Teikoku Kendo Kata* was published, and a proper written explanation of the *kata* devised. In May 1933 (*Showa* 8) the en-

Picture of prominent Kendo masters in front of the Butokuden building, Kyoto Taisho (4) 1915
Front left: *Shigesaburo Moyazaki, Goro Saimura, Moriji Mochida, Tadashi Monna, Takaharu Naito,*
Kuniharu Watanabe, Sosuke Nakano, Chikita Oshina
Second row: 2nd from left is *Kinnosuke Ogawa*, and others

Hakudo Nakayama performing *Hasagawa Eishin Ryu Iai* – sword drawing *Kata*. The demonstration takes place in front of the Emporer, *Showa*(15) in 1940.

This shows Goro *Saimura* in the *Seigan (Chudan) Kamae*.

larged annotation of the *Dai Nihon Teikoku Kendo Kata* was presented. It was at this time that it began to be known as the *Nihon Kendo kata*. In 1981 Select Committees met to study the original documents of the *Dai Nihon Teikoku Kendo Kata* and to discuss the possible revision and updating *Nihon kendo kata* by the documentation available. The first committee to make the draft consisted of five members: *Tatsuo Saimura* (Executive Director of ZNKR) *Noburu Shigeoka, Akira Sato, Yuji Onishi* and *Hideo Muto* (secretary ZNKR). It was then discussed by another committee with *A Sato* as chairman, and *K Nakakura, T Tokimasa, K Isaka, K Takigawa, T Kogawa, T Saeki, Y Onishi, Y Nishi, K Takashashi, M Komorisono, T Morishima, K Wada* and *M Osawa*. Another conference consisting of *K Horiguchi, S Ono* and *N Kojima* also discussed these matters. They found the edict difficult to understand. There was the possibility of misprints too, and it proved extremely hard to determine some of the exact technical explanations. It was decided then to take the *Dai Nihon Teikoku Kendo Kata* as it read, or they interpreted it, and change it into a more easily understood

A group of the prominent *Kendo* Masters in front of the *Butokuden* building in Kyoto, Taisho(4) 1915. The masters are:
Front centre – Takaharu Naito
Second row centre – Sosuke Nakano
Third row, third from the right – Yuji Taima, sixth from the right – Moriji Mochida.
Back row, first from the right – Kinnosuke Ogawa, second from the right – Goro Saimura.

An early *Showa* period (1926–1989) picture depicting *Kendo* Masters. In the centre is Dr. Kiji Tajimi. The front (left to right) shows Norimasa Kozeki, Sasaburo Takano, Hakudo Nakayama. The back (left to right) shows Kinnosuke Ogawa, Moriji Mochida, Sohachi Shimatani, Sosuke Nakano, Goro Saimura.

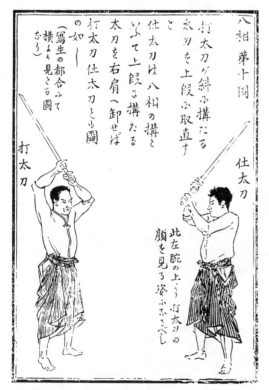

The *Hasso Kata* taken from the *Jikishin Kage Ryu No Kata*, published in 1901 by Meishin Saito.

15

language by reclassifying certain terms such as *seigan* to *chudan*, right and left *jodan*. The result was established as the *Nihon kendo kata* but it still remained in essence the '*Dai Nihon Teikoku Kendo Kata*'.

I would like to offer from the *Budo Hokan* of *Showa Tenran Shiai Huroku Dai Nihon Yuben Kai* (*kodansha* press 1930 showa 5) a translation of the philosophy of the *kata*, and some interpretation into the meanings.

UCHIDACHI
HANSHI (SASABURO   TAKANO)

SHIDACHI
HANSHI (HAKUDO   NAKAYAMA)
TACHI NO KATA

Each *KATA* means as follows:

DAI Ippon (the first)
Kamae of *AI-JODAN*, having *SEN*-attitude both move forward to each other, and then *SHIDACHI* wins by means of *SEN-SEN-NO-SEN*.

DAI Nihon (the second)
Kamae of *AI-CHUDAN*, having *SEN*-attitude both move forward to each other, and then *SHIDACHI* wins by means of *SEN-SEN-NO-SEN*.

DAI Sanbon (the third)
Kamae of *AI-GEDAN*, having *SEN*-attitude both move forward to each other, and then *SHIDACHI* wins by means of *SEN-SEN-NO-SEN*.

DAI Yohon (the fourth)
Kamae of *IN-YO-NO-KAMAE*, both move forward to each other, and then *SHIDACHI* wins by means of *GO-NO-SEN*.

DAI Gohon (the fifth)
Kamae of *JODAN* and *SEIGAN*, having *SEN*-attitude both move forward to each other, and then *SHIDACHI* wins by means of *SEN-SEN-NO-SEN*.

DAI Roppon (the sixth)
Kamae of *SEIGAN* and *GEDAN*, having *SEN*-attitude both move forward to each other, and then *SHIDACHI* wins by means of *GO-NO-SEN*.

DAI Nanahon (the seventh)
Kamae of *AI-SEIGAN*, having *SEN*- attitude both move forward to each other, and then *SHIDACHI* wins by means of *GO-NO-SEN*.

Ono Ha Itto Ryu Kata, with
Naritomo Tsurumi on the right
and Junzo Sasamori on the left.

Another display of *Ono Ha
Itto Ryu Kata*, with Junzo
Sasamori on the right and
Sasaburo Takano on the left.

Prize winners in *Showa*(4) 1929.
Mochida Sensei is in the centre
and Yokata Sensei is on the right.

先 先々の先 後の先

Sen – Stop your opponent's attack by first movement, forestall, attitude of taking the initiative. This does not mean speed, more subconsciously seeing the origin of every real action, or the practised ability to read a changing situation instantly. Having or assuming an advance intention of victory.

SEN SEN NO SEN – Anticipating your opponent's intention and capitalising on this knowledge to have victory.

GO NO SEN – Responding to your opponent's attacking movements by countering from them, without knowing your opponent's intention beforehand.

Reaction in *Sen Sen No Sen* and *Go No Sen* must be carried out at a faster speed than the actions of the attacker. Having a sincere and pure attitude of the single mind, unwavering and of a high and delicately refined quality. This is *Kigurai* and should be combined with *Sen* attitude.

Further definitions for *Sen*: Initiative, advantage, first-step and ambition.

Attitude . . . Position of the body indicating mood or emotion. Position can also be defined as proper place.

KODACHI NO KATA

Dai Ippon
Kamae: Uchidachi, Jodan, Shidachi, Chudan. Shidachi wins by rushing in and entering *Irimi Uchidachi* instantly. Feeling of *shin*.

Dai Nihon
Kamae: Uchidachi, Gedan, Shidachi, Chudan wins by provoking *uchidachi* and counter cutting. Feeling of *gyo*.

Dai Sanbon
Kamae: Uchidachi, Chudan, Shidachi, Gedan. Shidachi wins by thwarting and controlling every attack made by *uchidachi* without actually cutting him. Feeling of *so*.

These three feelings are somewhat different to the *sen* attitudes due to the differing sword length, although *sen* is applied throughout all the kata.

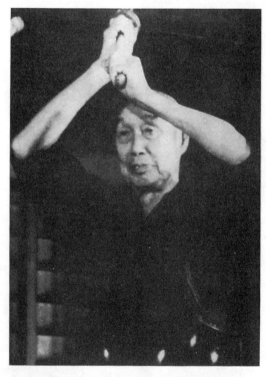

Moriji Mochida, in old age, demonstrates the *Jodan Kamae.*

18

An example of *Shinai Kendo* with Mochida Sensei on the right and
Nakano Sensei on the left. The scene is from the *Showa*(40) 1966.

A demonstration of *Nihon Kendo Kata* by Moriji Mochida
and Goro Saimura at the 1964 Tokyo Olympics.

眞
行
草

Further definitions:

Shin: Truth. Strike directly and attack strongly, rush in with the feeling of truth without fear and into *ten no kamae* showing true strength.

Gyo: Stream. Using your opponent's force, flowing like a stream with his attack, ensuring that you flow from the *men* cut into the final thrust. Movement is in a different direction.

So: Grass or weeds. Again blend with your opponent like blades of grass in the wind and move to make him work hard, tiring him by your multitude of movement like a field of grass. A million blades swaying in the wind; controlling but never retaliating. As grasses and weeds are among plants that come above ground in early spring, so your movement should also be before that of your opponent. *So* is also known as *kusa*.

Further comments on *shin, gyo* and *so*.

In *Renku* or *Haikai*, a sort of play in short poems, attaching a new piece of verse responding in accordance with the one made by another poet. In this sense *shin* is the way of using a style of verse exactly responding to the one made by another poet. *Gyo* is the not exactly responding

but almost in harmony with the former one. The last, *so*, is a style vaguely in response to the one made before. This way of *shin, gyo*, and *so* is also applied to *Kado* (flower arrangement) *Nihon Ga* (traditional Japanese painting) and *Zoen* (traditional gardening).

We can also determine that this style was also applied in the three forms of the *Koduchi Kata*, but the exact interpretation is somewhat obscure and one must draw one's own conclusions from this information into their meaning.

A PERSONAL INTERPRETATION

I would firstly like to offer a very simple interpretation which has been explained to me during my study of *kendo kata*. I have been extremely fortunate and privileged to study under many fine exponents, both here in Europe and on visits to Japan. It is well established that the *kata* which we practise today owes its origins to the *Seiho* or set training methods of the pre-*Tokugawa* era. However, the practice of *shinken shobu*, actual contest with only one survivor, the

A display of *Teikoku Kendo* Kata by Sasaburo Takano and
Hakudo Nakayama in *Showa* (4) 1929.

Kinnosuke Ogawa as a young man performing the cutting
technique on a straw bale.

other being despatched to a higher training hall
is definitely not the feeling or concept of the
kata.

This idea that *kata* is a practice for killing is a
misconception. True representation is the high
level training method as performed by two noble
beings, correct in posture, dress and attitude,
preparing to exact the practice of swordsmanship with true dignity and although both totally
committed to the technique, they work within
the dictated guidelines to the utmost of their
ability and control. It is a confrontation, with the

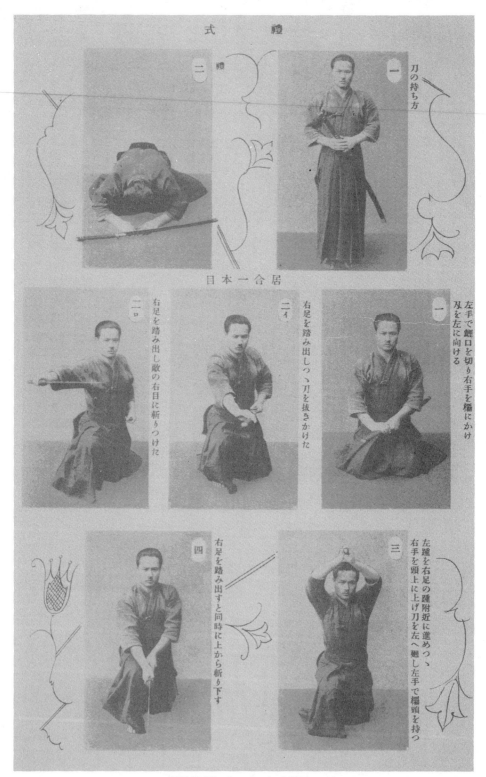

式　禮

1931 *Kinji Kaneko* performing *Iai Kata*.

resolve to carry it through to its conclusion. This conclusion is not stylised death with cuts that kill or pretend to. The feeling is of *uchidachi* as the teacher because he must lead *shidachi* through the *kata*. His sole purpose is to teach to the student the responses and techniques offered through his attack. Timing is created by *uchidachi*'s lead, thereby establishing the correct distance, the necessary responses and *zanshin* (awareness, unbroken concentration). To this end, it is necessary for *uchidachi* in each *kata* to strike or thrust at specific areas for *shidachi* to learn and practise the correct responses. Each response without ever actually following through by always stopping just short of bodily contact, clearly demonstrates the complete control and the technique. I will cover this in more detail within the technical section, but briefly there are set areas and cutting positions, depth of cut and related *kamae*. The most important part of *kata* must be the 'feeling', practising with true sentiment but in very simple terms.

Uchidachi instigates his attack with the feeling of 'This is what I am going to do.' '*Shidachi* responds: 'Yes, OK, just try it.' *Uchidachi* does. *Shidachi* counters: 'There, see what you'll get if you try,' and, with *zanshin* (awareness): 'Now try that again and I'm ready.' *Uchidachi*: 'Yes, I can see that, but, if you relax your awareness just a little, just once, then I'm ready to attack again.' *Shidachi*: 'I know that and I remain aware.' *Uchidachi*: 'Enough then, let's withdraw and begin again.' It is almost a feeling of 'I dare, you dare.'

This almost electric feeling is sometimes apparent in the highest level demonstrations by true exponents of the art. Keep your body strong by the correct use of breathing, *kiai* and awareness, and observe your opponent as a whole being rather than just watching his sword, feet or eyes. This Japanese term of '*Enzan no metsuke*' means looking at a far mountain (in simple terms: peripheral vision) or seeming to look and concentrate on, say, the eyes of your opponent. However, you actually observe every aspect of him, from the twitch of his little toe to the rise and fall of his breathing. You look at the whole of his existence past, present and future, so deep is this gaze of '*Enzan no Metsuke*'.

This is the essence of the *Kata*, making it a living, vital and realistic form. It is not the clockwork motion that unfortunately is often the nature of *kata* today.

Try to adopt *Enzan no Metsuke* at the start and although it is not always possible, try not to consciously look for too long at one area. It is important to attempt to cover the area with your spirit, as aptly demonstrated in *Kodachi Sanbon me*. The value of this approach is that as sight alone can be weak, the two-fold gaze utilises strong perceptive skills.

The use of *zanshin* awareness is further evidence to the control of technique. If *kata* were a practice for killing then there would be no need for *zanshin* as your opponent would be dead. It is rather the feeling of intensity in action through the practice of strikes and responses in the classical way, thereby learning swordsmanship through the varied predetermined forms. This is the interpretation of *kata* and it is more than mere physical practice, and not just the desire to be technically perfect even if that is attainable. Equally important too are the spiritual being, the sincere and pure attitude of the single mind, and the emotions of a delicately refined quality. The Japanese simply call this *Kigurai*, and at commencement of each *Kata*, the *Kigurai* of *Uchidachi* is at a higher level than that of *Shidachi*. As the *Kata* progresses, however, *Shidachi's Kigurai* rises and becomes greater than that of *Uchidachi*. Thus *Shidachi* ultimately overcomes *Uchidachi* by the stronger feeling.

To help understand this feeling of 'I dare, you dare', it is very useful to practise *kata* with *shinai* and wearing armour. Attack and counters can be modified to incorporate *Fumikomi Ashi* (stamping footwork) or *Okuri Ashi* (slidestep) and modified with techniques such as *Nuki*

Waza substituting this type of footwork for the backward or forward *Hidari Jodan No Kamae* (*zanshin* point) in the standard *Kata*. *Kote, men* and *do* are also applied, as well as the standard *kiai*. As well as presenting an updated form of *kata* this method is also a fine way of understanding the basic *kata* techniques and is of particular value in teaching.

Prominent Kendo masters.
Front left: *Sosuke Nakano*
Front right: *Kinnosuke Ogawa*, and others
Taisho (10) 1921 ·

24

ENZAN NO METSUKE

When walking in the countryside following a particularly well known and favourite route, it is possible to pass through the area without actually conscsiously looking at the various geographical features as you are so intent on reaching your destination. This is not to say that you do not see them, rather that you do not notice them. Likewise when arriving at a fork in the pathway, you automatically know which way to go without hesitation. One cannot say that the countryside is not noticed, but equally it cannot be stated that it is actively observed.

This effectively encapsulates the whole essence and intention of *Enzan no Metsuke. Ito Ittosai*, founder *Itto Ryu* 1560 to 1653, said, 'After all, when looking at mountains each has been seen'. So once seen never forgotten. With this in mind, one avoids taking the wrong pathway and is able to travel at will through all terrains.

So always remember the law of opposites, soft and hard, seen and unseen, responding accordingly. As these feelings exist within, so this is the way to gain victory over yourself and reach the far mountain.

Kinnosuke Ogawa in old age *IN NO KAMAE*

Nihon Kendo Kata 1960 *Showa* (35). Left is Moriji Mochida, and right is Goro Saimura.

25

The *Chudan no kamae*

Water

A middle level attitude focusing your point, *ken saki* to the point of your opponent's throat or *nodo*. This *kamae* is the best *kamae* for attack or defence. An every day *kamae*, regular posture, and suitable for all to use.

PHILOSPHICAL INTERPRETATION
Also known as *Jin* or *Nin no kamae*. Anybody or everybody's *kamae*, *hito kamae*, and ordinary person's *kamae*. *Chudan* is the *kamae* of water and can be called *mizu no kamae*. Hold your *bokken* still like a pool of water but not stagnant water, with an undercurrent watching, waiting and always covering. Protect yourself by being observant and calm, alive and waiting but fully aware. A positive *kamae*.

Note on *Chudan no Kamae* and *Mizu no kamae* (water stance). Be like water. Adapt to each different circumstance by being able to cast off fixed notions and fill the shape of each new vessel. From each set of sword patterns always be able to respond accordingly.

The *Jodan no kamae*

Heaven

A high level attitude with sword held raised above the head one fist forward parallel in line with your front foot. It can be (left) *hidari* or *migi* (right). If left then slightly turn your sword diagonally by the way your body is in the half turn of *Hanmi*. If right your sword is straight on to your opponent. Whether right or left *bokken* should be angled backwards at no more than 45°. This is classified as the expert's *kamae* or superior

stance in *shinai kendo*. It is common for a *kendoka* to excuse himself by saying 'go burei,' or 'Please excuse me for adopting this arrogant manner.' Classical schools say that in left *Jodan* your body should be straight to your opponent as in *Migi Jodan*, so that you cannot be caught off balance which can happen when assuming a turned posture.

PHILOSOPHICAL INTERPRETATION
Also known as *Ten no Kamae*. Looking down on your opponent from heaven, heaven *kamae*. Compared with the other four *kamae*, *Jodan* can be further defined as a *kamae* of total attack. Having a strong spirit and thinking nothing of defence, you have only to cut down with the sword. *Jodan no kamae* is therefore compared to the *kamae* of fire, which is very aggressive and burns everything. Ready to engulf your opponent by cutting him with fire, shooting outwards, burning him by the strength of your cut in a rush of flames. A positive *kamae*.

Gedan no kamae

Earth

Low level attitude focus your point approximately 5 to 6 cm below your opponent's knees.

PHILOSOPHICAL INTERPRETATION
Also known as *chi no kamae*, the *kamae* of ground or sand: earth attitude but nevertheless performed with strong spiritual bearing. It should have the same feeling as *jodan* and *chudan* but is more a *kamae* of defence in waiting, inviting. A negative *kamae*. Anciently *Gedan no kamae* was taken also when one had to fight with many enemies. When you take *Gedan no kamae* against your opponents *chudan no kamae* he will find it very difficult to attack. *Gedan no kamae* stops *chudan no kamae* and guards well.

Hasso no kamae

In

Sword raised point straight up with 45 degrees angle backwards. Laying *Tsuba* in line with your mouth one fist distanced, elbows relaxed, cutting edge directly facing your opponent. Angled back like *Jodan*. Left foot forward. The feeling of this *kamae* is to cut the shoulder or neck of your opponent.

PHILOSOPHICAL INTERPRETATION
Also known as *In no kamae* as a feeling of waiting or inviting your opponent to attack. Also known as *ki no kamae*. The *kamae* of standing like a big tree thrusting upwards to heaven, quiet yet firm, with roots deep under the ground. Cut by going through the *jodan* position like the rush of a falling tree, unstoppable. A semi positive *kamae*, almost neutral but more than half attack and less than half defence.

Waki gamae

Yo

Attitude where your sword is concealed behind you by stepping right foot back, half turned body, *hanmi*. Put the *bokken* down from your right hip, relax your right hand, grip left hand holding constant. Don't let your point be too high or too low, maintain your point about knee height. Draw back from a *chudan* and make sure your opponent can't see your sword. The focus cutting is under your opponent's arm in an upward motion, although this is not applied in these *kata*.

PHILOSOPHICAL INTERPRETATION
Yo no kamae, attacking *kamae* positive attitude, also known as *kin no kamae* or gold *kamae*: 'Hidden valuable.' You don't show your opponent your strength or your weapon. You can react as you wish. A positive *kamae*. *Yo* also means plus, or sunny side. The opposite to shadow.

In and *Yo* are also read as *Yin* and *Yang*: negative and positive or black and white opposites. *In* develops and creates *Yo*, so the universal laws exist. Autumn follows summer, night follows day, so the *kata* must be practised ceaselessly as only by constant effort can you master and be the victor of yourself. But even though you achieve this victory and become a master, always remember that humility, like the universe, is endless.

The *kamaes* are referred to as *go gyo*, five attitudes, five streams or currents and are the result of standardisation i.e. Basic responses left *Jodan*=right *jodan* or *chudan*. *Waki*=*hasso*, *gedan* to *chudan* or *gedan*. But they come from much wider origins and attitudes of mind that affect the connotation and application existing within the classical schools. Five streams, calm but alive, waiting but fully aware.

Finally, *kamae otoku* or falling *kamae*. This is the position in the close of each *kata* where both participants assume a mutual position of *Bokken* point at the opponent's left knee for mutual withdrawal. No advantage position. It means to break, drop or fall.

The speed of *kata* should not be too fast for if you rush you will make mistakes. Always try to get the *kata* to flow. At the other end don't be too deliberate in your movements. Try to achieve a good balance of movement, spacing and technique. Remember that a *kata* is a two sided learning process. If you make a mistake you may interrupt your partner's *kata* and then it becomes inoperative. The saying 'learn by your mistakes' in this case should be learning from continued application. Simply feel the movements happen, respond to your partner, move as one and reply to reaction as it happens with intent.

CHAPTER TWO

INTRODUCTION TO TECHNICAL SECTION – *NIHON KENDO KATA*

I hope this small effort will be of some assistance in the performance of *Kata*, its origins and interpretations, and that it may stimulate a revival of interest in *Kendo Kata*, and be of some help to beginners when learning the *kata*. The *kata* is performed with *bokken* to try and create the feeling of standard *Dojo* practice. After all, the *kata* is supposed to be a training method as one learns to execute the techniques and refine their usage by actual application and working movements. We have tried, therefore, to perform the *Kendo Kata* with as much reality as possible, and I have attempted to give some insight into the concepts that have previously been left unexplained and often unanswered.

Each *kata* can be divided into three sections:

1. The foot methods and *kamae* attitudes for bringing the two participants to the centre position.

2. The actual application of techniques from this centre position.

3. The foot method for withdrawal from the centre position together with the *kamae o toku* or breaking the *kamae* on completion of the technique.

TECHNICAL SPECIFICS

Owing to the variety and importance of Japanese terms, it will be necessary thoughout the technical sections to refer to the technical glossary.

Standard dress for *kata* is *Keiko gi*, the practice jacket, and *hakama* which is a divided skirt, and traditional dress. *Montsuki* and *Hakama* are worn formally, and on the back of the *Kimono*, the family heraldry is printed (*Mon*). For the purpose of this book we performed the *kata* without

Shizentai

Sizentai sage to grip

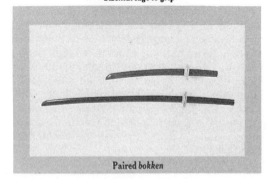

Paired *bokken*

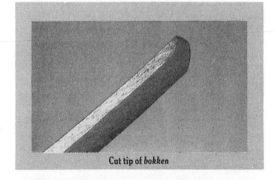

Cut tip of *bokken*

tare although the *kamae* are shown wearing this item. *Tare* are worn at examinations and seminars for identification purposes, often chalked with a reference number. *Keikogi* should be tucked in well with no creases in the back of the jacket. *Hakama* should be well pressed and not crumpled looking. This of course applies to all *kendo* practice.

Try to have a pride in appearance and a pride in practice will follow. For the purpose of *kata* practice a knot should be tied, an old sword knot, in the tapes of your *hakama* as illustrated. Bows and loops are not acceptable for the performance of *kata*. The *bokken* are wooden and in pairs; *tachi* refers to long sword, either wooden or metal and *Kodachi* is the short sword, again wood or metal. As a safety note, new *bokken* often have a sharp pointed end and it is well worth blunting this end by removing the point to avoid any unnecessary injury that may occur by accident. *Tsuba* or guard and a rubber retaining ring should always be affixed for practices, or an unnecessary injury could again result. When carrying *bokken* in the *dojo* prior to *kata*, hold in your right hand, not quite touching the *tsuba*

Hakama knot for kata

Sage to both

Gripping both for carrying

with the cutting edge facing back and upwards, with your arm by your side at full length with the point also behind you. *Sage to* is the term for this position. When carrying a pair in the right hand, have the *kodachi* gripped in the thumb and index finger in a circle; and with the *tachi* gripped in between index and middle finger. The *tsuba* of the *kodachi* should be under the *tachi*, therefore the *kodachi* is next to your body, point slightly raised above that of the *tachi* (SEE ILLUSTRATION)

Gripping both

REI – THE BOW

For the purpose of examination, the *rei* may be performed as follows:

Stand in natural position (*shizentai*), swords in the right hand, distance 9 steps apart from your partner and both turn to the direction of the *kamiza* and execute a deep bow from the waist, eyes focused on the floor about 3 metres in front of you. Turn back to your partner and bow, *o tagai ni rei*, at a lesser angle than that for *kamiza* but again from the waist, eyes focusing on your partner about the knee area but observing all of him in the '*Enzan no metsuke*' gaze.

Single grip for carrying or holding

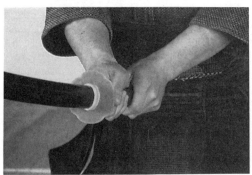

Kamae grip

Rei to partner

Rei, sage to grip to partner

Rei to kamiza

Change over grip

Change over

Taito

Taito

Sage to

Shidachi now turns and moves to a diagonal position to his rear right side, about 3 steps distance, and putting his right knee down in a kneeling position, lays the *kodachi* down, cutting edge inwards to his body, and left knee raised in the direction of the *kamiza*. Standing up he returns to his position opposite *uchidachi*, still holding his *bokken* in the right hand *sage to* position. Both now bring their *tachi* in front, although timing dictates a marginal time lapse of *shidachi* behind that of *uchidachi*'s movement to signify teacher and student. Transfer the *tachi* to the left hand again and take the *taito* position, with sword raised to a drawing position on the left hip.

It is best to stand with your thumb just below your navel, and at the *sage to*, changing over hands right to left, avoid touching the *tsuba* by your grip.

FOOT POSITIONS AND DISTANCES

Normal stance *shizentai*, with the feet together but not touching. The footwork for the purpose of the *kata* is that of *ayumi ashi*, or natural walking, but performed in a flowing controlled manner. Avoid bobbing and rising whilst moving forward and backwards or executing technique. The use of *okuri ashi* is limited to certain responses. *Hiraki ashi* is also used but *fumikomi ashi* stamping footwork is omitted. The stance of the feet, parallel with right foot forward and left foot behind and with the heel slightly raised, can be attributed to the secret teachings of *Ito Itosai* (1560–1653).

THE FOOT METHODS AS REFERRED TO IN THE *KATA* EXPLANATIONS

For a rule of thumb a movement is calculated as a three or five step distance by counting the first step as a small slide of the foot foremost in the intended direction of travel, i.e. forward three steps from the *chudan no kamae*, slide right (it should be forward), step left, step right. You should now be at the *Issoku Itto No Ma* stance with your partner's *bokken*. Five steps backwards from this position, slide left (this is your back foot), step right, step left, step right, step left. You should now be back where you started. Please note that the five small steps backwards must equal the three larger steps forwards, and maintain the separating distance of nine steps

Kamae stance

Front view of the *kamae* stance

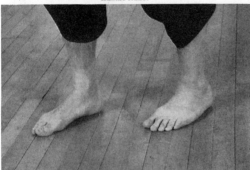

Avoid too wide a stance

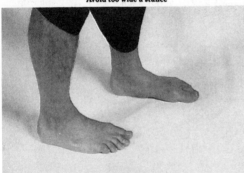

Avoid flat parallel stance

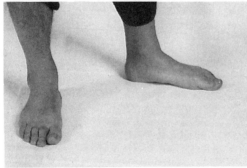

Avoid splayed flat foot positions

between *uchidachi* and *shidachi*, throughout the starting and finishing positions of each form within the *kata*.

The bodily posture should be one of an upright stance straight onto your partner, right foot forward, left foot behind, back foot left toe in line with right heel with normal space suitable to your build and height between the feet to ensure good balance, approximately 5 to 10 cm with both feet pointing in the same direction and the left heel raised to walk by pushing your body forward, not dragging by means of a front foot drawing movement. Move naturally with shoulders relaxed, back hollowed, hips down, and your *bokken* held in a *kamae* position with intent but not tensely, a proud posture ready for action. Regarding the height of your heel from the ground, and this applies to left and right *kamae*, one Japanese *sensei* explained it as follows: Imagine you have a mouth in your foot, just under your left heel. You need to breathe through this mouth. If your foot is down you cannot breathe and you suffocate. If your heel is too high you will be overcome by too much air. Maintain a position where this mouth can breathe normally. To help in this you can flex your knees, bending them slightly into a forward position. Then by this action it is easy to raise your left heel.

When gripping the *bokken* in *kamae* hold with the palms but gripping predominantly with the little and ring fingers. Try to avoid leaving a gap between *bokken* and palm. Have slightly bent elbows and maintain a stance with your neck straight and shoulders relaxed with no obvious power in them as your strength is in your hips. Hold your form as if you had an egg under each arm. Breathe with your stomach, quietly.

32

Maintain the *Enzan no metsuke*: eyes everywhere. This can also be further defined as long term viewing, gaining insight, a look that cannot be shortsighted. A further guide to the arm position in the *chudan no kamae* can be likened to holding a barrel or ball in your arms.

BREATHING AND *KIAI*

From assuming the *chudan no kamae* the *kata* has begun. At this point, take a deep breath into your stomach or *hara*, a point just below your navel (where life begins), or as deeply as you can and hold it. Move forward on the attack and counter. *Kiai* give voice to your breath, in other words exhale and shout. The *kiai* formulated to *yah* for *uchidachi* and *toh* for *shidachi*. These sounds were taken from the five basic sounds at the formulation of the *kata*. On the *kiai* do not allow all of your air to escape, hold a little back, enough to continue moving without inhaling. Complete the movements up to the *kamae o toku* falling *kamae* before you breathe in. If you cannot manage this, try to work it in stages without consciously showing that you are breathing in and out. Eventually you should aim for one breath, one *kata*; a sort of *kakari geiko* feeling of the all out attack in as few breaths as possible.

The *Butokukai* in their *Ten Chi Jin no kata* used the sounds *yay-eh, iya-toh* or *ei*. As recorded in the minutes of the 1932 meeting of the *Dai Nihon Kendo kata* committee of inquiry, it is recorded that the *kiais* decided on were *yah* and *eh*. However, a proposal was put forward by *K. Yano Sensei* to have *ya, eh* or *toh*. The result on the voting in this matter was decided as *yah* and *toh,* as they correspond to the breathing of *'a'* and *'un.'* In effect, *'a'* is the breath of attack (positive),

Tachi kamae otuku

Kodachi kamae otuku

Chudan

Migi jodan

Chudan Hamni against *Jodan*

Chudan Hamni against *Gedan*

Gedan kamae

Sonkyo

Sage to

Taito

Chudan

Left jodan

Gedan

and '*un*' the breath of defence (negative). Actual examples of these characteristics can often be seen in the faces of the statues of stone lion dogs (*Komainu*) which face each other at the entrance to *Shinto* shrines, guarding the precincts. In the practice of *kata*, the way to act and react is to grip and release. To grip is to absorb your opponent's spirit, and to grasp immediately. To release is to let go your own spirit immediately. Both of these happen in an instant and this is the way of the *Yah Toh Kiai* sequence of the *kata*. According to tradition there are five *kiais*: *iyeh, eh, yah, hah* and *toh*. *Yah* shows that one is mentally prepared. *Eh* or *Iyeh* is the *kiai* of boldly deciding the moment of attack and *toh* is made at the moment of counter attack. *Hah*, unfortunately has been lost in the mists of time. *Kiai* is the highest accord owing its existence to the action as a man's word and action occur spontaneously. An example would be as in *Shinai Kendo* to shout 'head' (MEN) and strike at the same time. The *Kiai* originated from the humblest of beginnings and has no designs or conceptions to constrain it.

DISTANCE OR *MAAI*

The distance at which you practice is an important link to the timing of the attack and the response. Timing is made by *uchidachi* and *shidachi*'s timing is a split second behind. If you like, it's a direct response to a movement. If this is executed at a distance too far between the two, then the *kata* becomes meaningless because the cut doesn't reach so therefore there is no necessity to respond, or, if a *shidachi* does respond, then this too is without substance or meaning, and results in no understanding of the interpretation. If the two are too close bad technique will result and incorrect execution of the

Hasso

Waki

kata is assured. By using the standard foot methods, a correct distance can be maintained for the commencement or conclusion of the *kata*. *Kata* should always start at the centre position from the *Issoku Itto* distance, *ken saki* (TIPS) just crossing.

Although not always obviously visible when watching the performance of *kata*, and in particular that at the highest level, there exists a series of signals or triggers that are of paramount importance in learning the cause and effect of the *kata*. Although it is stated that the controlling

Paired *shizentai* for rei 1

2

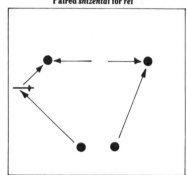

3

Lay down *kodachi*

3

4

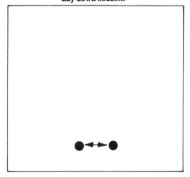

influence of the *kata* is made by *Uchidachi*, *Shidachi* has to get a reaction from *Uchidachi* in order to perform the correct movements.

Ipponme
From the right *jodan* position at the centre meeting point *Shidachi* makes a slight downward movement as if about to cut, hence causing *Uchidachi* to commit himself to the full blooded *men* cut. *Shidachi* then applies *nuki* to avoid this attack.

Nihonme
In the centre *chudan* position, *Shidachi* slightly raises his point or presses the *Uchidachi* sword to the left, almost as an invitation to *Uchidachi* to cut his *kote*, which he does.

Sanbonme
At the *chudan* position, raised from *gedan*, *Shidachi* comes up to *chudan* slightly later than *Uchidachi*, inviting *Uchidachi* to *tsuki*, or thrust.

Yohonme
After the *Aiuchi*, which should have the feeling of *Uchidachi* going into *jodan* and cutting (*Uchidachi* doesn't know the length so attacks) and that of *Shidachi* realizing and revealing now the length of his sword, reacting by cutting with a feeling of stop, into *aiuchi* (simultaneously cut) and then down into *chudan*. *Shidachi* relaxes his *kamae* slightly thus inviting the thrust of *Uchidachi*.

Gohonme
From the raised *chudan* (*seigan*), *Shidachi* pushes slightly forward *seme* with his *ken sen* towards the *kobushi* of *Uchidachi*, the left fist area of the left *jodan kamae* or opens his *Ken Sen* slightly right side. *Uchidachi* reacts by cutting *men*.

Ropponme
Shidachi applies pressure twice, firstly from *gedan* into *chudan* causing *Uchidachi* to back at speed into *jodan* and back further into *chudan*, and again by this feeling of pressure forcing *Uchidachi* to commit himself to a rather hasty *kote* attack.

Nanahonme
Shidachi again inviting a thrust by slightly raising his point and on the thrust, on upwards into a parry. *Aitsuki* (simultaneous thrust)

Kodachi Ipponme
Shidachi makes *Uchidachi* react by pressure of *seme* at the *kobushi* of *Uchidachi*, with the feeling or *Irimi*, (entering).

Nihonme
Shidachi, by trying to hold down the spirit (will) of *Uchidachi* and *Uchidachi* backwards into *waki gamae*, *Shidachi* forward again by *seme* and *irimi*, *Uchidachi* reacting *men* cut.

Sanbonme
Shidachi by *Gedan*, invites via this open unguarded position to cut his *men*, a welcoming invitation to attack.

It cannot be stressed enough that these signals should in no way alter the timing or tempo of the *kata*, as they are subtle movements that become less and less apparent as the practitioner becomes more and more fluent. In the final event they become part of the very feeling of the *kata*, invisible but integral. However, when first learning *kata* movements, they should not be made unless they are made apparent, as this establishes at a very early level this true cause and effect. Thus if no reaction is given to a situation, no action should be taken.

CHAPTER THREE

THE *KATA*

As this technical section of the book is designed to assist the beginner in the study of method and examination, it will again be necessary to refer to the terminology and some of the previous headings.

Mutual Interpretation

Rei, as explained, change *bokken* from right to left hand, from *shizentai* (natural standing). Take three steps toward your partner using the 3-step method. As you arrive on your right foot in the third step, simultaneously take the *tsuka* (handle of your *bokken*) and pull it forward slightly, then continue to draw it completely out, assume the *sonkyo* position with your right knee slightly forward but with both knees parallel in height and your back in an upright position. Now, both rise without adjusting your feet, to the *chudan no kamae* position in the distance of *Issoku Itto No Ma*. Now just turn your left foot to a position parallel to the right as mentioned in the bodily posture. Make *kamae o toku* (falling *kamae*) and withdraw using the 5-step method, and prepare to begin by assuming the *chudan no kamae* attitude in readiness for the first form. From here do not make any unnecessary forward movements or foot adjustments, slight foot slides or otherwise. Remain on the exact spot that you finished on after the 5-step withdrawal.

FORMAL COMMENCEMENT

Enter the area with *uchidachi* in front, *shidachi* behind and carrying *bokken* in your right hands. Stand side by side, *rei* to *kamiza*. Standing, move to a position opposite each other about three steps apart. *Seiza* with your *bokken* and lay them on the floor to your right side but *Shidachi* lays *kodachi* nearest to his body, *tsuba* in line with the knee, cutting edge facing your body.

Shidachi start   S1

Make a deep *rei* with both hands down to the floor simultaneously, forefinger and thumb touching to form a triangular space with the other fingers touching. *Shidachi's* bow should be slightly lower than *uchidachi* to give respect to the teacher. Both stand with *uchidachi* walking to a position to his rear, slightly to the diagonal right about nine steps. *Shidachi* walks to a position to his rear, more diagonal of about seven steps, lays down his *kodachi*, stands up and moves two to three steps diagonally to face *uchidachi* at the nine step distance.

S2

S3

S4

5

6

S9

S8

38

With *bokken* in the right hand, *sage to, rei* and change to thumb on *tsuba* to left *taito*. Using the 3 step method come to the *sonkyo* and begin. At *kata* finish, reverse the procedure and leave the area. Calculate the three or five step distance by counting the first step as a small slide of the foot foremost in the intended direction of travel, i.e. forward three steps from the *chudan kamae* slide right (it should be forward), step left, step right. You should now be at the *issoku itto* distance with the *bokken* in your hands. Five steps backwards from this position, slide left (this is

Uchidachi start   U1

U4

U3

U2

7

your back foot), step right, step left, step right, step left. You should now be back where you started. Please note that the five small steps backwards must equal the three larger steps forwards, and maintain the separating distance of nine steps between *uchidachi* and *shidachi* throughout the starting and finishing positions of each form within the *kata*. There are of course slight variations within some of the *kata*, but these are covered within the technical explanations of each *kata*.

U8

U9

Heaven

S1

S2

S3

IPPON ME –
THE FIRST LONG SWORD *KATA*

Shidachi

Breathing in, your timing marginally behind that of *uchidachi*, respond to his *hidari jodan* assume the *migi* (RIGHT *jodan no kamae*). Move forward to the centre position using the 3-step method whilst still in the *jodan no kamae* and allow a slight pause as a direct response to that of *uchidachi*.

Now avoid *uchidachi's shomen* attack by simultaneously drawing your hands back and upwards and moving your body backwards by *okuri ashi* foot method, thus allowing *uchidachi's bokken* to pass down in front of you. (*Nuki waza*) Bring your *bokken* down and execute a *shomen* cut together with *okuri ashi* foot forward movement with *kiai toh*. As *uchidachi* attempts to move away by half step, as if seeking an opportunity to continue, bring your point down to focus on the centre of his face (between the eyes). As *uchidachi* moves back a further half step, still looking as if testing your

4

6

8

Heaven

U3

U2

U1

Uchidachi

Breathing in, step forward on your left foot and assume the *hidari* (LEFT) *jodan no kamae*, with a slight pause to allow *shidachi* to assume his *kamae*. Now using the 3-step method take three paces forward and pause at the central position looking for the opportunity to attack. Seizing the moment, cut *shidachi's shomen*, including his raised hands, head and body, cutting right down to a *gedan* level in a semi-circular fashion and *kiai yah*. After *shidachi's* counter cut, take a half step backwards by *okuri ashi*. Again take a half step backwards testing his *zanshin* and maintaining your own, foot movement by *okuri ashi* and watching constantly for possible lapses in his concentration whilst never relaxing your own. When *shidachi* has assumed the left *jodan no kamae*, count to four in your head. This is the *zanshin* timing before finishing the *kata*. Begin to raise your *bokken* from its lower level position

5

7

9

Heaven

zanshin to the full, step forward on your left foot, assume the left *jodan* and assert your *zanshin* fully from this position. As *uchidachi* begins to raise his *bokken* step back with your left foot and meet his point with yours in the *chudan* position at the *issoku itto* distance, still maintaining strong concentration. Make *kamae otuku* and withdraw using the 5-step method. Now assume the *chudan no kamae* in readiness for the next form.

10

12

S14

S13

Cut fully down

Guidance note for *Shidachi* and *Uchidachi*

Try to avoid a too far back or leaning position of the *bokken* in *jodan*. Due to the *migi jodan* position of *shidachi*, it is perfectly feasible for *uchidachi* to make the initial cut full blooded in an attempt to cut hands, *bokken* handle, (*tsuka*) head and body, and missing *shidachi* only by his *nuki* evasion technique. The cut travels through to the *gedan* position. *Uchidachi's* cut should be an outward curved movement, full and beautiful in its application and avoided by only minimal evasion on the part of *Shidachi*.

Uchidachi may adjust the distance so two steps may equal one step. This occurs when attempting to back away after *shidachi's* counter but always maintaining good posture.

11

as held after the failure of the initial attack, meeting his point with your point in the *chudan kamae* at the *issoku itto* distance. As he also assumes the *chudan no kamae*, still maintaining full *zanshin* throughout, make *kamae otuku* and withdraw using the 5-step method.

Now assume the *chudan no kamae* attitude in readiness for the next form.

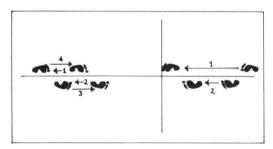

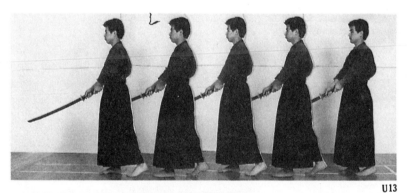

U13

U14

Avoid this position when performing *Nuki Waza*

Avoid these positions (*kamaes*)

Water

S1

S2

NIHONME –
2ND LONG SWORD FORM

Shidachi

Breathing in as a response to *uchidachi's* movement, move forward to the *issoku itto* distance using the 3 step method in the *chudan kamae*. On *uchidachi's kote* attack, drop the point of your *bokken* to the *gedan* position and at the same time step back with your left foot to the diagonal left side of *uchidachi*, bringing your right foot so that you are diagonally to the right of *uchidachi*. Swing your *bokken* under his cut and up as a counter cut from overhead. *Kiai toh*.

3

5

7

水
Water

U2

U1

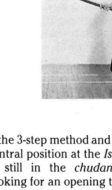

4

6

8

Uchidachi

Breathing in, use the 3-step method and advance forward to the central position at the *Issoku itto* distance. Whilst still in the *chudan kamae* attitude, pause looking for an opening to attack. Seize the opportunity and cut to *shidachi's kote* by lifting the *bokken* to almost the *jodan* position and making a big cut directly to *shidachi's* right wrist. The cut finishes in a position slightly lower than *shidachi's* right wrist, as if you had cut or made contact. *Kiai yah* with the feeling of having just cut into the wrist, cutting by right foot *okuri ashi* (slide step). On the completion of *shidachi's nuki* technique, counter cut maintaining strong concentration and again counting to four in your head (timing point). Bring your *bokken* under that of *shidachi's*, sliding back by *Okuri Ashi* footwork, left foot first, still keeping strong concentration as you move, make *chudan* with *shidachi* meeting in the centre position at the *issoku itto* distance. With your point, make *kamae otuku* and withdraw using the 5-step method. Now assume the *chudan no kamae* in readiness for the next form.

水
Water

and finish with your cut just above the right wrist of *uchidachi*. Right foot and cut should be carried out simultaneously with the performing of the *nuki* by footwork and by lowering of your hands.

As *uchidachi* begins to move back bringing his *bokken* under yours, maintain your concentration by keeping good *kensen* to *uchidachi's* centre and step back to the centre position making *chudan* with *uchidachi* in the *issoku itto* distance. Make *kamae otuku* and withdraw using the 5-step method. Now assume the *chudan no kamae* in readiness for the next form.

9

S11

S10

Guidance note for *Shidachi* and *Uchidachi*

Uchidachi should avoid cutting *kote* so that the *bokken* finishes in the *gedan* position as this position is too low. *Shidachi* should try to avoid curling the *nuki* technique and try to drop the point straight down, allowing the weight of the *bokken* to achieve this with minimal effort. Then move to the side (because although the cut has been evaded, the point is still alive) and directly in front. Make sure the movements flow from the evasion to the counter cut as one timing. Both should try to cut in an upward and outward circular fashion; a cut in a beautiful arc-like movement.

A

B

水
Water

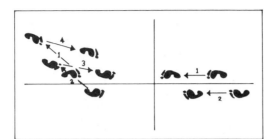

U10

U11

C

D

E

F

S1

S2

S3

SANBONME –
THE 3RD LONG SWORD FORM

Shidachi

Breathing in, respond to *uchidachi's gedan* by making your own *gedan kamae*, using the 3-step method to meet *uchidachi* in the centre position, point to point. With strong feeling, respond by raising your *bokken* until *uchidachi* attempts his *tsuki*. On his attempt, slide your body back using the *okuri ashi* method. Calmly deflect *uchidachi's* thrust with the top edge (*shinogi*) of your *bokken* and turning it in your hands so that the cutting edge faces to your right, *ire zuki ni nayasu*. With *uchidachi* committed to *tsuki*, counter thrust using the *okuri ashi* foot movement and thrust with a straight *bokken* into the centre of *uchidachi*. *Kiai toh* and stepping forward after the attempt by *uchidachi* to hold

4

6

8

地
Earth

U3

U2

U1

5

7

9

Uchidachi

Breathing in, assume the *gedan no kamae* attitude and use the 3-step method to meet *shidachi* in the centre position, point to point just crossed. With strong feeling start to raise your point from the *gedan no kamae*, feeling for an opportunity to thrust into *shidachi*. Seizing this opportunity and using *okuri ashi* footwork, thrust by turning your *bokken* so that the curve of the *bokken* goes round that of *shidachi's kamae*, with the cutting edge out to your right side. *Kiai yah* and thrust into *shidachi's* stomach. Seeing your attack spoiled and *shidachi* countering with a straight thrust, step back with your right foot behind and try to maintain a *chudan no kamae* at this point by focusing your *kensen* on the throat of *shidachi*. *Shidachi* does not have full control of the centre and as he steps in again with *seme*, you feel that if you stop, his *bokken* will push through your body because this *seme* is so strong. Withdraw whilst still trying to make *chudan* by stepping back again on your left foot. *Shidachi* now has 60% control to your 40% so continue withdrawing by sliding left, right, left, finishing right foot forward. Retract with dignity but still exercise strong concentration so that if *shidachi* were to relax there centre *kamae* on your initial trust, step through onto the left foot with a strong *seme*, a feeling of if your opponent were to stop you would push your *bokken* through him. (*Kurai seme*) and continue forward to step right, left, right to finish with your *bokken* to the centre of *uchidachi's* face (between the eyes). Hold this position *zanshin* until *uchidachi* begins to raise his sword. Begin to withdraw by sliding left, step right, step left. Your point now meets that of *uchidachi's* with both raised to the *chudan no kamae*, keeping the *Issoku itto* distance. Continue stepping back, step right, step left and finish in the *chudan no kamae* with your right foot forward. Make *kamae otuku* and withdraw using the 5-step method. Now assume the *chudan no kamae* in readiness for the next form.

10

13

15

S19

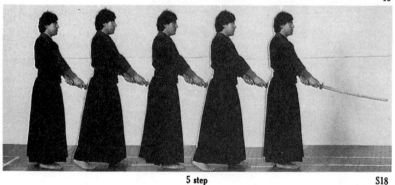

5 step

S18

地
Earth

11

12

14

may still be the chance to counter. With *shidachi's zanshin* (*bokken*) point in the centre of your face, hold your own *zanshin* though you leave your hands down to the right, count to four (timing point) in your head, and begin to raise your point up. On *shidachi's* third step backwards, meet his point in the *chudan no kamae*, *Issoku itto* distance and continue moving together by sliding right, step left, step right. Make *kamae otuku* and withdraw using the 5-step method. Now assume the *chudan kamae* in readiness for the next form.

16

17

5 step   U18

U19

Guidance note for *Shidachi* and *Uchidachi*

Shidachi Avoid doing two *tsuki*. A feeling of one *tsuki* and then strong *seme*, entry with intent, should suffice. Don't rush the movement as the footwork is quite complex for both sides. Feel each other's timing and learn to harmonise. When learning the footwork patterns allow good pauses and timing. In the final return to the centre position as a beginner it is acceptable for *shidachi* to do the steps as three and two. However, the better your understanding and performance of the *kata*, the more it should have a feeling of five flowing steps and a joining

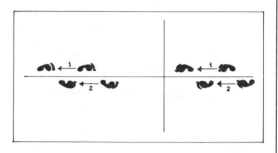

Tsuki point *uchidachi*

Tsuki point *shidachi*

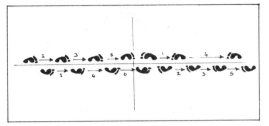

together. The initial feeling after *shidachi's* counter thrust is one of *uchidachi* trying to maintain centre. At this stage the feeling is more or less equal on both sides with no advantage to either.

As *shidachi* steps in again with a strong *seme*, the feeling is of a slight advantage to *shidachi* over *uchidachi*. *Uchidachi* then chooses to withdraw in a *kamae otuku* like position but never allowing his concentration to relax at any time.

Both should start from *gedan* with strong spirit of looking for an opportunity to attack, as there is no opening *suki*, as both are in *gedan no kamae*, in addition to the fact that it is hard to attack directly from *gedan no kamae*. On receiving *uchidachi's* initial thrust, *shidachi* should avoid bending his arms or bringing his left hand off from the centre line of the body. A good distance is essential through footwork and sword tip control. *Uchidachi* on receiving and parrying the *tsuki* and *seme* of *shidachi*, maintains a position so that *shidachi's* point would pass your body and not into it.

Position of point on the advance of *shidachi*,
Finishing up focussed between the eyes.

Gold

S1

S2

S3

S4

5

YOHONME –
THE 4TH LONG SWORD FORM

Shidachi

Breathing in on *uchidachi's hasso* attitude, step back on your right foot and assume the *waki Gamae*. Taking three smaller than usual steps forward, slide left, step right, step left and pause. As *uchidachi* assumes *jodan* respond likewise. Cut strongly and quickly, meeting the *bokken* of *uchidachi* in the same attitude both locking,

7

9

Tree

U3

U2

U1

6

U4

Uchidachi

Breathing in, step forward on the left foot and assume the *hasso no kamae*. Take three smaller than usual steps forward and by using the 3-step method, slide left, step right, step left, pause and pass through the *jodan kamae* (*hidari*) cut strongly to the head of *shidachi*, thus meeting the stopping movement from *shidachi*. In the feeling of *kiri musubi* a simultaneous cut with *bokken* locking, *shinogi to shinogi*. Draw down to the *chudan no kamae* at the *issoku itto* distance, adjusting the distance by sliding *okuri*

8

10

金
Gold

11

shinogi to shinogi. (*Kiri Musubi.*) Draw down to the *chudan no kamae* maintaining good concentration. *Uchidachi's tsuki* and its force throws your blade to your right side and you push up your hands in the feeling of, as children joke when they do this technique, 'wiping your nose upwards'. Simultaneously with the *maki kaeshi* movement step to your left side by moving your left foot diagonally across and keeping it behind the right. Now move forward by stepping forward onto your left foot and deliver a big cut to the *shomen* of *uchidachi*. *Kiai toh* and as *uchidachi* begins to raise his *bokken* to the *chudan no kamae* maintain good concentration and return to the centre position, meeting his *bokken* in the *issoku itto* distance *chudan no kamae*. Make *kamae otuku* and withdraw using the 5-step method. Now assume the *chudan kamae* in readiness for the next form.

14

16

S18

S17

12

13

15

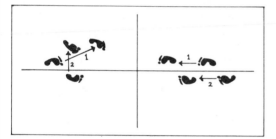

ashi if required. Maintaining good strong concentration, you feel the opportunity to thrust (*tsuki*) into *shidachi's* right lung (position of the bow on the *keikogi* will do as a marker) by using the curve of the *bokken* to get round the *kamae* of *shidachi*. Using *okuri ashi* slide right foot forward. Due to the deflection of *maki kaeshi*, your body should be inclined slightly forward indicating a full commitment. *Kiai yah* and as *shidachi* counters with *maki kaeshi* and makes his *shomen* cut, count to four in your head (timing point) and step back. *Okuri ashi* and assume the *chudan no kamae*, meeting *shidachi's* point in the centre position at the *isoku itto* distance. Still keeping good concentration make the *kamae otuku* and withdraw using the 5-step method. Now assume the *chudan no kamae* in readiness for the next form.

U17

U18

Tree

Avoid cutting into each others *bokken*.   Cut straight

Cut high *Aiuchi*

Avoid

... or your opponent can cut you.

58

金
Gold

3

4

7

8

Tsuki point

Ensure a closeness to your body with your *bokken*.

Guidance note for *Shidachi* and *Uchidachi*

Shidachi should maintain good contact on the right side whilst in the *maki kaeshi*, thus avoiding leaving a gap that *uchidachi* could penetrate and cut the exposed right side. Ensure the final cut is from above the head and not from the shoulder. *Shidachi* must ensure that his *waki Gamae* conceals the weapon and its length behind him and is in the correct position for cutting when taken through the *jodan* attitude. Both should avoid cutting into each other's *bokken*, instead cut directly and straight. The feeling is of both strongly cutting to *shomen*, so strongly that your *bokken* lock together, remaining in this *aiuchi* position. Now draw down into the *chudan kamae* with intent. *Shidachi's* reaction to the initial attack from *Uchidachi* is one of 'no you don't, stop!' A swift counter cut and into *aiuchi*: the simultaneous strike.

S1

S2

S3

GOHONME –
THE 5TH LONG SWORD FORM

Shidachi

Breathing in as a response to *uchidachi's jodan*, focus your point on his left fist area (*kobushi*) and face behind. This is still referred to as *chudan* but is sometimes known as *seigan no kamae*. Formally this *kamae* was specified as *Hiraseigan*, although the term is no longer used. Slightly angle your *bokken* by turning the cutting edge inwards to the left, thus protecting your right *kote*. Using the 3-step method move to the

4

6

8

U3

U2

U1

Uchidachi

Breathing in assume the left *jodan no kamae*, (*hidari*). Using the 3-step method move to the centre position and pause. Feeling the opportunity to cut *shidachi's shomen* step forward on the right and cut. *Kiai yah* and on the deflection of *suriage* by *shidachi*, allow your *bokken* to drop down to a *gedan* level position, whilst still maintaining good concentration. As *shidachi* moves into the *hidari jodan* after the *men* cut, count to four in your head (timing point), and bring your *bokken* to the *chudan no kamae* meeting with *shidachi* at the *issoku itto* distance. Move back to the centre position leading *shidachi* by 3 small steps. Slide left, step right, step left. Make *kamae otuku* and withdraw using the 5-step method. Now assume the *chudan no kamae* in readiness for the next form.

5

7

9

Water

centre position and pause. On *uchidachi's*
shomen attack lift your *bokken* straight up and
deflect his cut by *suriage*, simultaneously
moving your body backwards by *okuri ashi*
method. *Uchidachi's bokken* is thrown down by
the force of your *suriage* to a central *gedan*-like
position, allowing you to counter cut *shomen* to
the head of *uchidachi*. *Kiai toh* and stepping
back from this cut, assume the *hidari jodan* with
an action of bringing your point down from the
shomen to the centre of *uchidachi's* face
between the eyes, step back into the *hidari jodan*
no kamae with strong *zanshin* and in one
flowing movement. As *uchidachi* raises his
bokken to the *chudan no kamae*, step back on
your left foot and assume the *chudan no kamae*
meeting his *bokken* in the *issoku itto* distance.
Follow *uchidachi* to the centre position using the
3-step foot method. Make *kamae otuku* and withdraw using the 5-step method. Now assume the
chudan no kamae in readiness for the next form.

10

13

15

S18

S17

天
Heaven

11

12

14

16

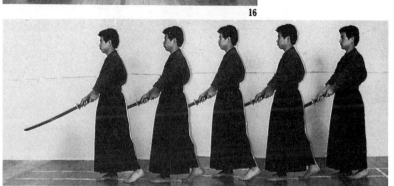
U17

U18

Guidance note for *Shidachi* and *Uchidachi*

It is worth noting that this *kata* contains one of the areas of specific attack, for it may appear that the *shomen* attack of *uchidachi* does resemble the cut of *Ipponme*. However, if this is applied, it will result in the striking of *shidachi's tsuba* and the performing of a poor *suriage*. The actual cutting point is only as deep as the chin of *shidachi* and allows good *suriage* to be performed. On receiving *suriage* allow your *bokken* to fall or be thrown down to the *gedan* level centre position by this action. It is also very important for *shidachi* to combine good hand and body movement to achieve a good reaction. Do not over-react in the upward deflection of *uchidachi's* cut as the movement of *suriage* is very subtle. At the moment when *uchidachi's* hands squeeze as he grips or just before *uchidachi's men* cut arrives is the best timing.

It is also worth noting that because of the attitude of *chudan* as angled to cover the *kobushi* and protect the *kote* of *shidachi*, the options open for attack by *uchidachi* would seem to be limited to this chin deep *shomen* cut.

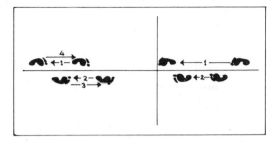

Uchidachi cuts no deeper than to the chin.

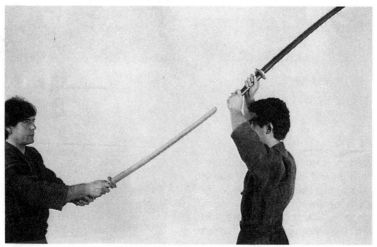

Cover the *Kobushi* but at a long distance.

Too deep a cut by *uchidachi* results in
Striking the *Tsuba* in *suriage* technique.

Earth

S1

S2

S3

ROPPONME –
THE 6TH LONG SWORD FORM

Shidachi

Seeing that *uchidachi* is maintaining his *chudan no kamae*, breathe in and assume the *gedan no kamae*. Using the 3-step method, move to the centre and begin to threaten through your rising *kamae* the centre of *uchidachi* just below his *ko bushi* (fist), with the feeling of if *uchidachi* doesn't move you'll thrust into him with the feeling of strong *seme* by strong will. Your pressure causes *uchidachi* to move back quickly into *hidari jodan* and you move forward with a strong *seme* but resisting the temptation to thrust due to his raised *jodan no kamae* (but still maintaining strong pressure throughout).

Maintain *chudan no kamae* with strong concentration but as *uchidachi* also moves back into this *chudan no kamae* because of your strong pressure, he suddenly strikes at your *kote* with a *chisai*, or small cut. Respond with a small *suriage* at the same time as stepping onto your left back foot diagonally to the right side of *uchidachi*. Stepping into line with your right foot, cut his *kote*, again *chisai* (small action) from the actions of continuous *suriage kiai toh*. As *uchidachi* moves diagonally to your right and slightly away from you, step after him by assuming the *hidari jodan* with strong concentration. As *uchidachi* begins to move forward to the centre position step back and assume the *chudan no kamae*, meeting his *bokken* in the *issoku itto* distance in the centre position. Make *kamae otuku* and withdraw using the 5-step method. Now assume the *chudan no kamae* in readiness for the next form.

4

6

8

水
Water

U2 First position held

U3

U1

5

7

9

Uchidachi

Breathing in, maintain *chudan no kamae* and use the 3-step method and move to the centre position. Feeling the strength and pressure of *shidachi's* rising *kamae*, quickly step back into *hidari jodan* but with a slightly shorter distance between the feet, more like a half stance. Maintain good concentration as *shidachi* follows you with his *seme* movement, stopping at the threat of your raised *jodan*. Now assume the *chudan kamae* by stepping back on your left foot. With strong concentration, assume the *chudan no kamae* (under pressure). You have no option but attack and cut by *okuri ashi* right foot forward, a small cut to the *kote* of *shidachi* (*chisai kote*). *Kiai yah* and on the *suriage* deflection of *shidachi*

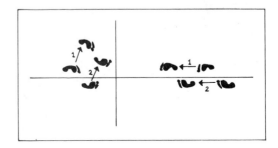

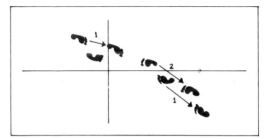

地
Earth

10

11

14

15

S19

S18

Guidance note for *Shidachi* and *Uchidachi*

Try to keep good distance as the sequence of movements is punctuated with fast and slow technique. A good co-ordination is desirable in the performance of the *kote* cut and *suriage*: try to deflect smoothly and with a small movement. Avoid the temptation to do *fumikomi ashi* (stamping cut) on the small attack by *uchidachi*, and use a side step, or (*Hiraki Ashi*) instead.

Shidachi must maintain strong and continuous pressure on *uchidachi*, forcing him to react and allowing him no chance to settle.

Suriage

水
Water

12

13

16

17

U18   U19

Thrusting point

step back by *okuri ashi* to your diagonal left and
looking at *shidachi* with good strong concentration, bring your *bokken* to a position with the
cutting edge facing right side down. Count to
four in your head (timing point) and move back
to the centre position in three steps right, left
right. Assume the *chudan no kamae* and meet
shidachi's bokken at the *issoku itto* distance in
the centre position. Make *kamae otuku* and
withdraw using the 5-step method. Now assume
the *chudan no kamae* in readiness for the next
form.

S1

S2

NANAHONME –
THE 7TH LONG SWORD FORM

Shidachi

Maintain the *chudan no kamae* and breathe in. Using the 3-step method come to the *issoku itto* distance centre position and meet with *uchidachi*. As *uchidachi* attempts a *tsuki*, push your *bokken* forward and upward to the shoulder level at the same time as pushing your hands forward. This deflects *uchidachi's* thrust

3

5

7

Water

U2

U1

4

6

8

Uchidachi

Maintaining the *chudan no kamae*, breathe in. Using the 3-step method come to the *issoku itto* distance centre position meeting *shidachi* and pause. Looking for the opportunity via threatening with a thrust into the breast of *shidachi* (*kiatari*) using the curve of your *bokken* to get round the *bokken* of *shidachi*, slightly, turning it to get round the point of *shidachi* and pushing your body slightly forward by *okuri ashi* method. On the upward deflection of *shidachi* assume the *chudan no kamae* with the feeling of

Water

by a locking process. Simultaneously strike *aitsuki* and slide your body and feet by *okuri ashi* method in a slight backwards direction. With a good concentration respond to *uchidachi's chudan* by also assuming the *chudan* at the *issoku itto* distance. As *uchidachi* attacks *shomen* by the 3-step method, slide your right foot slightly to alter your direction in relationship to *uchidachi's* oncoming body diagonally to his left (your right side). Step in forward on the left foot and cut into the right *do* (SIDE) of *uchidachi* with a diagonally downward cut. *Kiai toh* and continue forward diagonally, step right and pull the *bokken* through without contact and out in an extended arm position with the cutting edge away from *uchidachi* and the point parallel to the floor. Move through into a *sonkyo* like attitude to finish in a kneeling position with the right knee on the floor and the left raised knee facing *uchidachi*. Continue to look at him with strong *zanshin*. As *uchidachi* turns to face you, and assumes *jodan* respond likewise, bringing your right foot to straighten in line with your left raised knee in the kneeling position, whilst adopting this kneeling *jodan no kamae* and down into *chudan* to meet his *chudan* in the *issoku itto* distance, still kneeling on the floor. As *uchidachi* moves backwards, rise up as if being drawn up by his movement and

9

12

14

16

17

水
Water

10

11

13

15

18

strong concentration. Feeling an opportunity to attack the *shomen* of *shidachi*, slide right foot, and lift your sword well over head and continue forward stepping left and right to cut full blooded to a *gedan* level position. On the last right step *kiai yah* on the *shomen* cut. On *shidachi's* counter-cut and movement turn your head and look at *shidachi*. Count to four (TIMING POINT) and assume *waki* type *kamae* by just twisting your hips and body to face *shidachi*. Do not step, but still maintain strong concentration. Move into the *hidari jodan* position and down into the *chudan* by stepping back on your left foot. Using the *okuri ashi* method move back and harmonise with *Shidachi* as he rises from his position on the floor in the *chudan* kneeling position to a standing *chudan* in the *issoku itto* distance. Now return to the centre position through seven steps, maintaining the *chudan no kamae* in *issoku itto* distance with strong concentration.

This series of movement is in a circular formation. From the *chudan no kamae*, assume the *sonkyo* position, *osame to* your *bokken*. Stand up and withdraw by using the 3-step method holding your *bokken* level. (*Taito*). At the 9-step distance *shizentai* in a natural stance, change your hand on your *bokken* and thumb on *tsuba* to right held hand and down to the right *sage to* level. *Rei* and wait for the return of *shidachi*.

73

Water

step through and up onto your right foot. Maintain *issoku itto* in the *chudan kamae* and move with *uchidachi* back to the centre position in seven continuous steps in a circular formation. Assume the *sonkyo* position, *osame to* to left *taito*, stand up and withdraw using the 3-step method. At the 9-step distance change hands with the thumb on the *tsuba* to the right held *bokken* in the *sage to* level and *Rei*.

19

22

23

S28

S27

S26

S29

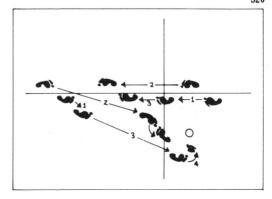

水
Water

20

21

24

25

U26

U27

U28

U29

水
Water

In the *Nanahonme* 7th long sword form, on cutting *nuki do*, *shidachi* must avoid lifting the right hand so that it is higher than the left. *Kiai* should be made with no pause between, i.e. *yah-toh* not *yah*, pause *toh*. When returning to the centre position on completion by the seven continuous step circular method, avoid crossing over your feet or jerky stopping movements. Rather flow and remain alert.

At the nine step distance *bokken* in right hand, *sage to*, *rei* and change to thumb on *tsuba* to left *taito*.

1

4

5

8

9

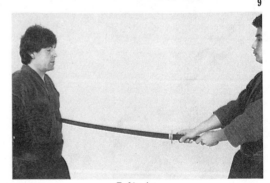

Tsuki point

水
Water

2

3

6

7

10

11

Do cut

Kneeling *kodachi* down   1

Kneeling *Tachi* down   2

Kneeling both *bokken*   3

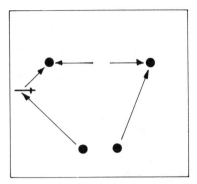

Rei and turn to walk three steps diagonally backwards to the right of your starting position where you have placed your *kodachi*. Kneel down with the right knee to the floor and place the *tachi* on the floor. Pick up the *kodachi* in the right hand, turn around and return to the starting position.

Paired *bokken*

KODACHI KATA COMMENCEMENT

From *sage to rei* to *uchidachi*, change hands as previously by taking left and take the 3-step method to the centre. Draw the *kodachi* with the right hand and, making *issoku itto* distance, place your left hand on your left hip with your thumb facing backwards. Now make *kamae otoku* by lowering the point of the *kodachi* at *uchidachi*'s knee. At the same time move your left hand down to your upper thigh, the thumb touching the index finger with the other fingers

closed, and withdraw to the 9-step distance using the 5-step method. Assume the *chudan no kamae* by focusing on the *nodo* or throat of *uchidachi* with your point.

S1 S2 S3 S4

5 6

S9 S8

80

When waiting for the return of *shidachi*, *uchidachi* usually rests in the *sonkyo* position. *Rei*, change hands right to left as before. Take the 3-step method to the centre, draw the *bokken* and assume the *chudan no kamae*. Make *kamae otuku* and withdraw using the 5-step method to the 9-step distance. Now assume the *chudan no kamae* in readiness for the next form.

U4

U3

U2

U1

7

U8

U9

Shin

S1

S2

S3

KODACHI IPPONME –
1ST SHORT SWORD FORM

Shidachi

From the *chudan no kamae* and in response to the *jodan* of *uchidachi*, breathe in and assume the *chudan hanmi kamae*, focusing your point on the centre of *uchidachi's* face. In response to *uchidachi's* initial movement use the 3-step method to move to the centre position maintaining good concentration, with the feeling of

4

6

8

U3

U2

U1

Uchidachi

Breathe in and assume the *hidari jodan no kamae*. Using the 3-step method move to the centre position and pause. As *shidachi* movement forward is of a threatening feeling, attack his *shomen* as in *tachi gohonme* allowing the *bokken* to fall down to a *gedan* level position. *Kiai yah* when stepping through on the right foot

5

7

9

irimi. As *uchidachi* cuts *shomen* from the left
jodan, enter with this feeling of *irimi no seme*:
wanting to enter directly into *uchidachi*. Using
the technique of *uke nagasu* deflect the cut of
uchidachi making minimal contact at the point
of the *kodachi* in this action. Turn to face
uchidachi by bringing your left foot in line with
the right, maintaining an *okuri ashi* stance. Cut
shomen, *kiai toh* and move back by *okuri ashi*
method. Assume a *jodan no kamae* feet by the
okuri ashi method left right. As *uchidachi* turns
to you and begins to raise his *bokken*, maintain
good *zanshin* and meet his point in the *chudan
no kamae* without any foot movement. Move
back to the centre position by again stepping
diagonally left right to make *issoku itto* distance.
Make *kodachi kamae otuku* and withdraw using
the 5-step method. Now assume the *chudan no
kamae* in readiness for the next form.

10

12

14

S17

S16

84

11

on deflection of *shidachi* look at him, maintaining good strong concentration and count to four (timing point). Turn to him by moving your right foot and bring your *bokken* to *chudan* in this diagonal position, meeting with his point in the *chudan no kamae*. Stepping back to the centre by moving your feet *okuri ashi* left right and still maintaining good *zanshin* in the *issoku itto*, *chudan no kamae*, make *kamae otuku* and withdraw using the 5-step method. Now assume the *chudan no kamae* in readiness for the next form.

13

15

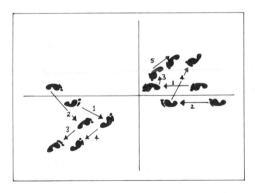

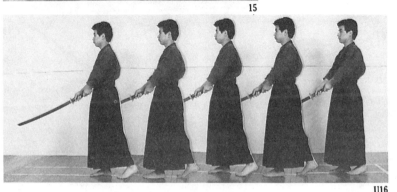

U16

U17

Guidance note for *Shidachi* and *Uchidachi*

Try to avoid strong contact on your *kodachi* in the performance of the *uke nagashi* movement. Rely on your foot movements *ashisabaki* and your bodily movements *taisabaki* to avoid the cut of *uchidachi*. In this *kata* you perform *chudan* at the finish whilst in diagonal facing position before you return to the centre starting point. Variable speeds are important such as a fast deflection by the *uke nagasu* but slower on the *shomen* counter cut and when moving into the *jodan no kamae* to show your *zanshin* (WITH STRONG INTENTION).

Minimal contact

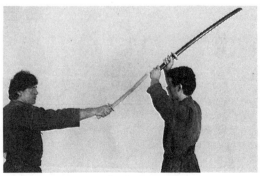

Focus point

真

2

3

6

Make good position

Avoid

87

Gyo

S1

S2

S3

KODACHI NIHONME –
2ND SHORT SWORD FORM

Shidachi

Breathing in, assume the *chudan hanmi kamae* keeping the *kensen* on the chest area of *uchidachi*. Using the 3-step method come to the centre position with your *kodachi* still covering the *gedan no kamae* of *uchidachi*. As *uchidachi* begins to raise his *bokken*, angle your point slightly downwards trying to restrain the upward movement by pressure without contact. As *uchidachi* steps back on his right foot into *waki gamae* level as response from your *irimi seme*, move forward with this feeling of *irimi no seme* and bring your point to throat level of *uchidachi*. As *uchidachi* steps forward cutting *shomen*, step by *hiraki ashi* method to his right side. Deflect his cut by *uke nagashi* with minimum contact to

4

6

8

U3

U2

U1

5

Uchidachi

Breathing in, assume the *gedan no kamae*. Move to the centre position using the 3-step method. Begin to raise your *bokken* from the *gedan no kamae*. As you feel the pressure, strong concentration and *seme*. By the movement of *irimi* from *shidachi*, step back on your right foot taking your *bokken* to the *waki gamae* and continue with flowing movements via a *jodan* position, step through on your right foot and cut into the *shomen* of *shidachi*. *Kiai yah* and allow your

7

9

行

Gyo

your *kodachi* using *ura shinogi* (right side of the upturned blade) and continuing the cut *shomen* from above your head. *Kiai toh.*

Slide in further to grip *uchidachi's* right arm at the elbow in a sort of holding down, almost pushing movement or restraining action whilst still maintaining good contact and strong concentration. At the same time bring your *kodachi* right down to your right hip, turning it inwards with the cutting edge out diagonally facing away from you and thus you show *zanshin* by threatening *uchidachi's* throat with your point from this hip level position. Feel *uchidachi's* timing signal indicated by his moving back slightly, and with strong concentration move back to the centre position. Keeping your sword point to the centre of *uchidachi*, make *issoku itto* distance and meet *uchidachi* in the *chudan no kamae*. Make *kamae otoku kodachi* and withdraw using the 5-step method. Assume the *chudan no kamae* in readiness for the next form.

10

13

15

17

18

11

12

14

bokken to continue down to the *gedan* level position. When *shidachi* has completed his *uke nagashi* and arm hold as a restriction to your lifting up again, count to four in your head (timing point) and move back slightly, thus giving the finish signal. Maintain strong concentration and bring your *bokken* up to meet *shidachi's* in the *chudan no kamae* at the *issoku itto* distance. Make *kamae otoku* and withdraw using the 5-step method. Assume the *chudan no kamae* in readiness for the next form.

16

19

行
Gyo

20

21

S23

S22

Guidance note for *Shidachi* and *Uchidachi*

By using a long step to the diagonal right of the centre line, bring your left foot behind and adjust your stance by moving your right foot to assume *okuri ashi* stance. Remember the *uke nagashi* is the action of pushing your right hand into a high level attitude with the feeling of brushing your nose by its closeness to your face. Avoid hard contact to your *kodachi*. Maintain the restraining action with a strong concentration onto the elbow joint of *uchidachi* in a downward holding motion. Try to force *uchidachi* into attacking through your forward *seme*; a response of pure reaction.

A

B

92

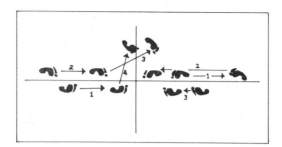

U22
U23

C
D
E
F

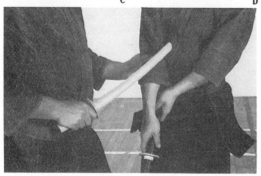

Sanshin position

Avoid

草
So

S1

S2

S3

KODACHI SANBONME – 3RD SHORT SWORD FORM

Shidachi

Breathing in, assume the *gedan no kamae*, and move forward in response to *uchidachi*'s walking approach attack. Bring your *bokken* straight up to receive the *shomen* attack of *uchidachi* with the feeling of *suriage*, thus stopping his cut and with a downward motion (*suri otoshi*), throw the sword of *uchidachi* down to his right side, maintaining your point in a forward position to a height of his right hip. As *uchidachi* steps in attempting to cut your right side, enter *irimi* on your left foot and using your body in a turning motion away from *uchidachi*, cut down with a flat angled *kodachi* toward the point of his *bokken, surinagasu*.

4

6

8

94

U3

U2 First position held

U1

Uchidachi

Breathing in, move forward in the *chudan no kamae*, attack *shidachi* to his *shoman* by slide step right, step left and begin to lift your *bokken*. Step right, lift up through the *jodan* attitude and cut *shomen* into high level position, high above the head of *shidachi, kiai yah*. On feeling the *suriage* contact with *sidachi's kodachi* and feeling his throw down or *suritoshi*, try to turn this to your advantage by taking your *bokken* through to your right side whilst keeping your right foot forward. Assume the *jodan* attitude as you cut through to the right *do* of *shidachi* by step cutting forward on your left foot. *Kiai yah*. As

5

7

9

Gripping his right arm with your left hand at the elbow, reverse your blade edge so that your cutting edge is on the side of his blade and positioned at 90 degrees. Slide it up to his *tsuba surikomi* and make contact with your *tsuba* to form a cross block and locking his elbow with your left hand grip, twist outwards to restrict the possibility of his counter cutting your legs. *Kiai toh.* As you execute the technique *surikomi* coordinate your body movement by gripping and locking his elbow with your left hand and *kiai* at this point, thus making good *ki ten tai ichi*.

10

13

15

17

18

11

12

14

shidachi's control *surinagasu* and *surikome* followed by the arm lock, makes you unable to move forward. Try to retreat, although still under pressure from *shidachi*. Slide backward right, step left, step right (left foot forward), and count to four in your head (timing point). Push forward slightly to signal *shidachi* to move back to centre and as *shidachi* completes his *zanshin* and withdraws, bring up your *bokken* to meet him in the centre position at the *issoku itto* distance.

16

19

97

So

As *uchidachi* tries to retreat, maintain strong concentration and follow, keeping close contact control. Pushing slightly, slide left, step right, step left, still holding good *zanshin* by moving your *bokken* to your right hip, turning it and using the point to focus on the centre of *uchidachi's* throat as before. On feeling the push of *uchidachi* signalling the end of *zanshin*, move from this position back to the centre position. Stepping from the diagonal, step left, right, left, meeting the *chudan no kamae* of *uchidachi* in the *issoku itto* distance.

20

23

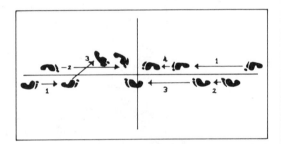

Suriage

Surinagasu

21

22

24

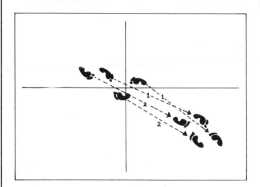

Surikomi

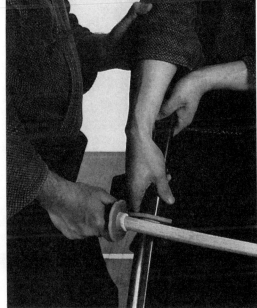

Lock *tsubas* and arm

99

草
So

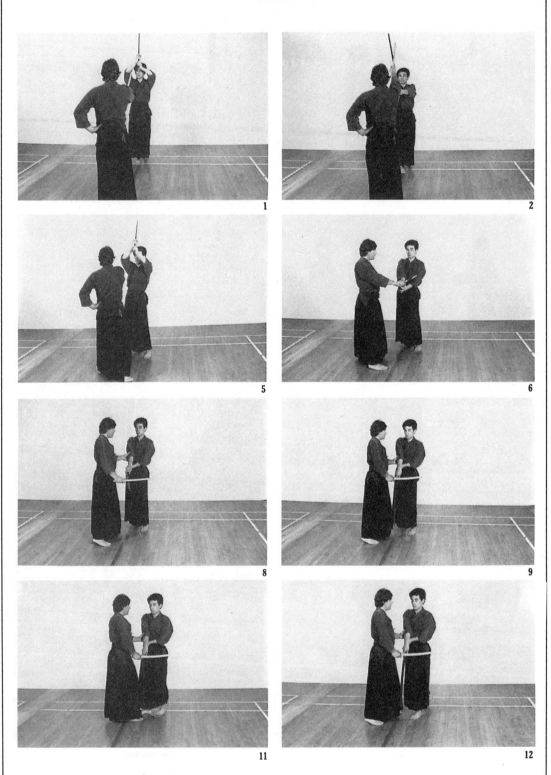

1

2

5

6

8

9

11

12

3

4

7

Avoid bad position

10

13

Cut is too deep

14

15

S20

S19

S18

S21

Sonkyo, osame to and withdraw. Change hands to the right, thumb on *tsuba, sage to* and *rei.* Now move back to the diagonal position where your *tachi* is on the floor and retrieve in the prescribed manner. Leave the area, still holding both *kodachi* and *tachi* in your right hand in the *sage to* position and with the prescribed forefinger grip.

16

17

U18

U19

U20

FORMAL *KATA* FINISH

Using foot method, slide left, step right to centre distance, *sonkyo, osame to* and withdraw using the 5-step method. Change hands to *sage to, rei*, and leave the area.

U21

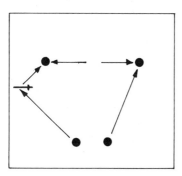

Formal *rei seiza*

Formal *rei seiza*

Formal *rei seiza*

Start and finish position paired.

SOME ALTERNATIVE PATTERNS OF PRACTICE

Single pairs

From the centre position, complete 1 to 7 *Tachi* and 1 to 3 *Kodachi* omitting the 5 and 3 step foot methods and also the *Kamae otoku*. Returning to the centre position in the *chudan no kamae* for the recommencement.

With *Shinai*

Using the same procedure for commencement, but with free movement to the side and back and forward. *Uchidachi* looks for the opportunity to attack but not immediately. A test of *Shidachi's* readiness.

With *Shinai* and Armour

(as previously mentioned in the technical section)

Group practice

2 and above pairs. Full application inc. 3 and 5 step foot method and *Kamae otoku*, but at this point informal *Rei* to your partner and move to your right or around to line up with a new partner. If odd numbers then one person resting as in standard *Mawari Keiko*. Rotate the practice in lines.

Circular formation

Form a circle around a central controller who will determine the *Kata* as *Uchidachi* or *Shidachi*. Perform the designated *Kata* with a new partner each time. The reverse can also be practiced, the outside practitioners of the circle selecting *Kata* and position. Both of these methods can be practiced with 3 or more persons.

With continuing practice a greater understanding of the *Kata* together with these types of application can prove to be interesting and extremely beneficial in the interpretation and application of predetermined sword techniques.

Hand Print Scroll from Ten Ran Shiai competition in front of the
Emperor in 1940.
Main prints of hands are of
   Sasaburo Takano
   Goro Saimura
   Hakudo Nakayama
   Moriji Mochida
   Kinnosuke Ogawa
Other writing is from practioners and competitors.

愛知　加藤喜右門

廣島　森求弘程

東京　小澤豊吉

長野　大楠哲爱

朝鮮　堀切源一

德島　高島永吉

東京　小城幽睦

東京　小野十生

無下　質四三雄

福岡　江藤小郎

大阪　坡川秀峰

群馬　岩越正

神奈川　横松揚之郎

神々　早坂房道

東京　増田東助

東京　兰木玉三

熊本　浅子沼郎

東京　柴田万葉

東京　泰回文南

京東　江邑叩吉

朝鮮　近藤智善

廣島　坜正平

石川　藤井鵰陀

九廣　宙山可洋

京都　若林伝治

剣道教士

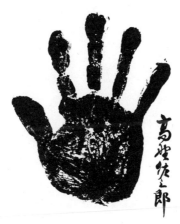

紀元二千六百年奉祝天覧武道大會出場選士

劍道範士　中野宗助

劍道範士　田本三郎

劍道範士　大麻勇次

劍道範士　高段茂戎

劍道範士　堀本統陽

劍道教士　伊藤精司

劍道範士　堀田捨次郎

劍道範士　海连崇

劍道範士　宗像養吉

劍道教士　白土留彦

劍道教士　山本忠次朗

静岡　劍道教士　杉山和民

京都　劍道教士　四戸泰助

京都　劍道教士　津崎菓敬

京都　劍道教士　田中知一

京都　劍道教士　大森小四郎

NOTES ON THE KENDO SCHOOL CHART

A Chart of the Schools and Branches influential in the Standardisation of Kendo Kata.

Some of the names date back to the 16th century, and continue through to the *Showa* period.

All school names are those contained within brackets.

1. (TENSHIN SHODEN SHINDO RYU)
IISHINO CHOISAI IENAO

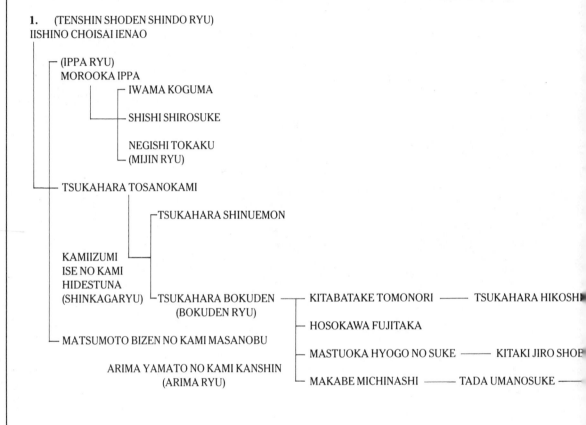

- (IPPA RYU)
  MOROOKA IPPA
  - IWAMA KOGUMA
  - SHISHI SHIROSUKE
  - NEGISHI TOKAKU
    (MIJIN RYU)
- TSUKAHARA TOSANOKAMI

KAMIIZUMI
ISE NO KAMI
HIDESTUNA
(SHINKAGARYU)
- TSUKAHARA SHINUEMON
- TSUKAHARA BOKUDEN
  (BOKUDEN RYU)
  - KITABATAKE TOMONORI ——— TSUKAHARA HIKOSHI
  - HOSOKAWA FUJITAKA
  - MASTUOKA HYOGO NO SUKE ——— KITAKI JIRO SHOE
  - MAKABE MICHINASHI ——— TADA UMANOSUKE ———

- MATSUMOTO BIZEN NO KAMI MASANOBU

ARIMA YAMATO NO KAMI KANSHIN
(ARIMA RYU)

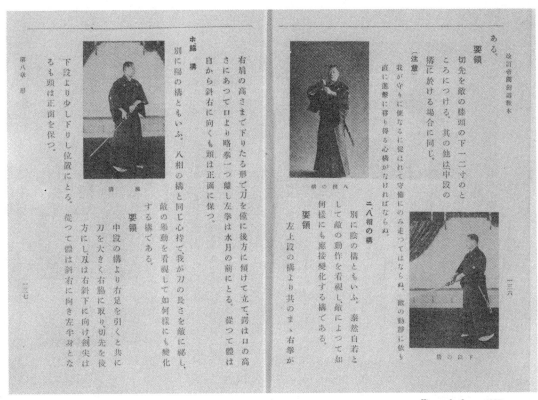

Kinnosuke Ogawa 1937
Waki Gamae
Hasso no Kamae
Gedan no Kamae

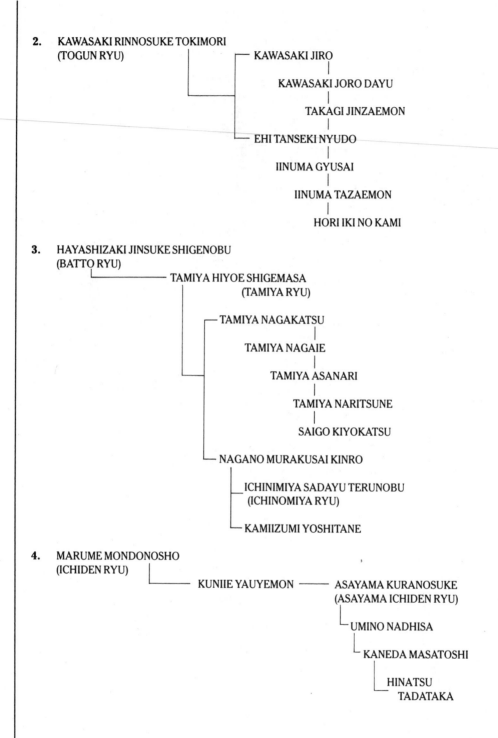

2. **KAWASAKI RINNOSUKE TOKIMORI**
   (TOGUN RYU)

   KAWASAKI JIRO
   |
   KAWASAKI JORO DAYU
   |
   TAKAGI JINZAEMON
   |
   EHI TANSEKI NYUDO
   |
   IINUMA GYUSAI
   |
   IINUMA TAZAEMON
   |
   HORI IKI NO KAMI

3. **HAYASHIZAKI JINSUKE SHIGENOBU**
   (BATTO RYU)

   TAMIYA HIYOE SHIGEMASA
   (TAMIYA RYU)

   TAMIYA NAGAKATSU
   |
   TAMIYA NAGAIE
   |
   TAMIYA ASANARI
   |
   TAMIYA NARITSUNE
   |
   SAIGO KIYOKATSU

   NAGANO MURAKUSAI KINRO

   ICHINIMIYA SADAYU TERUNOBU
   (ICHINOMIYA RYU)

   KAMIIZUMI YOSHITANE

4. **MARUME MONDONOSHO**
   (ICHIDEN RYU)

   KUNIIE YAUYEMON ——— ASAYAMA KURANOSUKE
   (ASAYAMA ICHIDEN RYU)

   UMINO NADHISA

   KANEDA MASATOSHI

   HINATSU
   TADATAKA

110

5.

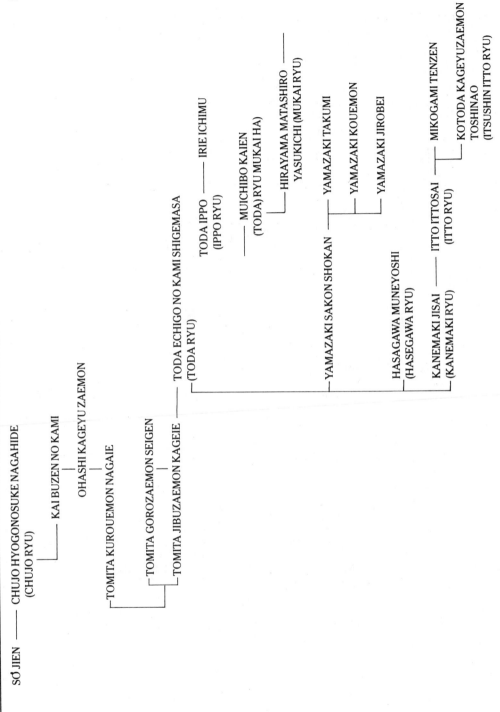

SŌ JIEN —— CHUJO HYOGONOSUKE NAGAHIDE
(CHUJO RYU)
└── KAI BUZEN NO KAMI

OHASHI KAGEYU ZAEMON

┌── TOMITA KUROUEMON NAGAIE
│
├── TOMITA GOROZAEMON SEIGEN
│
└── TOMITA JIBUZAEMON KAGEIE —— TODA ECHIGO NO KAMI SHIGEMASA
(TODA RYU)
├── TODA IPPO —— IRIE ICHIMU
│   (IPPO RYU)
│   └── MUICHIBO KAIEN
│   (TODA) RYU MUKAI HA)
│   └── HIRAYAMA MATASHIRO ——
│   YASUKICHI (MUKAI RYU)
│
├── YAMAZAKI SAKON SHOKAN
│   ├── YAMAZAKI TAKUMI
│   ├── YAMAZAKI KOUEMON
│   └── YAMAZAKI JIROBEI
│
├── HASAGAWA MUNEYOSHI
│   (HASEGAWA RYU)
│
└── KANEMAKI JISAI —— ITTO ITTOSAI
    (KANEMAKI RYU)   (ITTO RYU)
                        ├── MIKOGAMI TENZEN
                        └── KOTODA KAGEYUZAEMON
                            TOSHINAO
                            (ITTSUSHIN ITTO RYU)

111

6. KAMIIZUMI ISE NO KAMI HIDETSUNA

YAGYU TAJIMANOKAMI MUNEYOSHI
(SHINKAGE RYU)

YAGYU MATAEMON MUNETOMO
(YAGYU RYU)

YAGYU JUBEI MITUYOSHI

ATOBE GUNAI

ARAKI MATAEMON

YASUMARU CHUEMON KATSUYOMI
(KOKKI RYU)

NATSUMI ZOKU NO SUKE
(MUTAITAISHIN RYU)

WAKANA CHIKARA TOYOSHIGE
(TAIHEI SHINKYO RYU)

YAGYU MUNEFUYU

YAGYU MUNEHARU

YAGYU MUNEARI —— MUNENAGA —— TOSHIHIRA

TOSHIMUNE —— TOSHINORI —— TOSHIMUTSU —— TOSHIHISA

SHODA KIHEI (SHODASHIN RYU)

KIMURA SUKEKURO

IDEBUCHI HYONEI

TOKISAWA YAHEI (TENSHIN RYU)

YAGYU (HYOGO) TOSHIYOSHI —— YOSHIKATA —— YOSHITOMO

YOSHINOBU —— YOSHIKORE —— YOSHICHIKA —— YOSHINAGA

YAGYU GOROUEMON

MURAYAMA SAKUEMON MUNETSUGU —— MOCHIZUKI HAYATO
MASAYOSHIKATSU

KUBO SAKUJURO
IEYOSHI

Sasaburo Takano and *Hakudo Nakayama* from the *Budo Hokan-*
Showa-Ten Ran Shiai Huroku Dai Nihon. Yuben Kai 1930

7.

This shows Goro Saimura in the Seigan (Chudan) Kamae.

ITO ITTOSAI KAGEHISA
(ITTO RYU)

KOTODA KAN KAIUZAEMON TOSHINAO
(ITSUSHIN ITTO RYU)

KOTODA NIUEMON TOSHISHIGE

KOTODA YAHEI TOSHISADA

ZENKI

MIKOGAMI TENZEN TADAAKI

ITO TENZEN TADANARI
(ITTO RYU TADANARI HA)

KAMEI HYOUEMON TADAO

ITO TADAKAGE

ITO TADATSURA

NEGORO KUHACHIRO SHIGEAKI

HORIGUCHI TEIZAN SADAKATSU

MAMIYA GOROBEII HISANARI

MIZOGUCHI SHINGOZAEMON MASAKATSU
(MIZOGUCHI HA)

ITSUMI YOSHITOSHI
(KOGEN ITTO RYU)

FURUYA JIROZAEMON NOBUTOMO

IKUTA SYOEI —— FURUHASHI YOSHIMI

ONO JIROUEMON TADATSUNE
(ITTO RYU ONO HA)

ONO TADAYOSHI —— ONO NORIO

NAKANISHI SHIJYO —— NAKANISHI SHISYO

ASARI YOSHINOBU

ASARI YOSHIAKI

YAMAOKA TESSHU
(ITTO SHODEN MUTO RYU)

CHIBA SHUSAKU NARIMASA
(HOKUSHIN ITTO RYU)

MORI YOZO

CHIBA EIJIRO

WATANABE SOUEMON

WATANABE MATSUTARO

OZAWA SANJIRO

OZAWA TORAKICHI

MONNA TADASHI

NAITO KOUJI

TAKANO MITSUMASA

TAKANO AKIMASA

TAKANO YOSHISABURO

TAKANO SASABURO

KAJI SHINZAEMON MASANAO

HARADA TOSHISHIGE

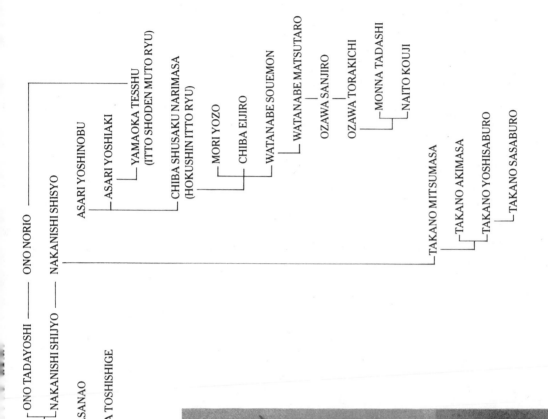

This shows Goro Saimura in the Seigan (Chudan) Kamae.

8. FUKUI HYDEMON YOSHIHIRA
(SHINDO MUNEN RYU)

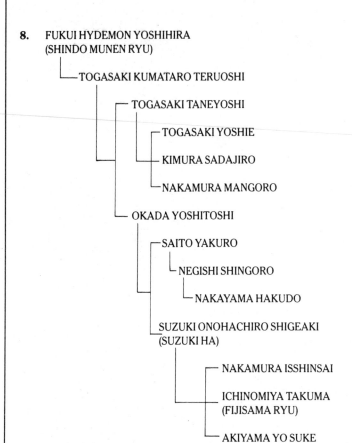

TOGASAKI KUMATARO TERUOSHI

TOGASAKI TANEYOSHI

TOGASAKI YOSHIE

KIMURA SADAJIRO

NAKAMURA MANGORO

OKADA YOSHITOSHI

SAITO YAKURO

NEGISHI SHINGORO

NAKAYAMA HAKUDO

SUZUKI ONOHACHIRO SHIGEAKI
(SUZUKI HA)

NAKAMURA ISSHINSAI

ICHINOMIYA TAKUMA
(FIJISAMA RYU)

AKIYAMA YO SUKE

9. AISU IKO
(AISU IN RYU)

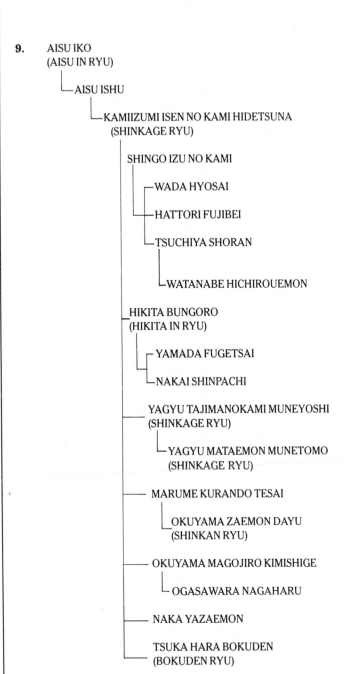

└─ AISU ISHU

    └─ KAMIIZUMI ISEN NO KAMI HIDETSUNA
       (SHINKAGE RYU)

SHINGO IZU NO KAMI

┌─ WADA HYOSAI

├─ HATTORI FUJIBEI

└─ TSUCHIYA SHORAN

    └─ WATANABE HICHIROUEMON

HIKITA BUNGORO
(HIKITA IN RYU)

┌─ YAMADA FUGETSAI

└─ NAKAI SHINPACHI

YAGYU TAJIMANOKAMI MUNEYOSHI
(SHINKAGE RYU)

    └─ YAGYU MATAEMON MUNETOMO
       (SHINKAGE RYU)

MARUME KURANDO TESAI

    └─ OKUYAMA ZAEMON DAYU
       (SHINKAN RYU)

OKUYAMA MAGOJIRO KIMISHIGE

    └─ OGASAWARA NAGAHARU

NAKA YAZAEMON

TSUKA HARA BOKUDEN
(BOKUDEN RYU)

117

10.

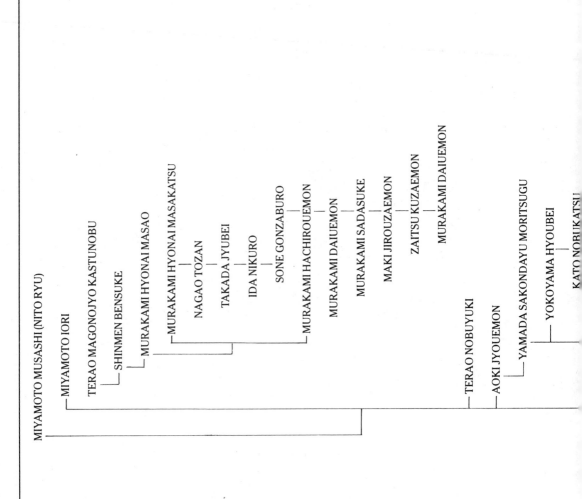

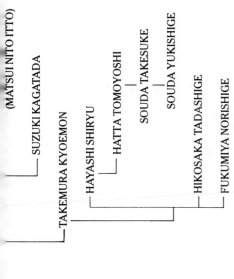

(MATSUI NITO ITTO)

SUZUKI KAGATADA

TAKEMURA KYOEMON

HAYASHI SHIRYU

HATTA TOMOYOSHI

SOUDA TAKESUKE

SOUDA YUKISHIGE

HIKOSAKA TADASHIGE

FUKUMIYA NORISHIGE

THE KENDO TEACHING SYSTEM

Until 1956 the system was a progression through the *Dan* levels to 5th *Dan*, and thence to specific grades:

1st *Dan*-5th *Dan-Renshi-Kyoshi-Hanshi*; the top grade.

Then in 1957 the system came under revision and more *Dan* levels were added from 5th, taking the *Dan* series to 10th level but retaining the teaching classification of *Renshi, Kyoshi* and *Hanshi*:

1st *Dan*-5th *Dan*-6th *Dan*-7th *Dan*-8th *Dan*-9th *Dan*-10th.
Renshi   Kyoshi   Hanshi

Kendo Masters Biography

Noboru Watanabe b. April 1838 d. 10 November 1903

From the *Shinto munen-Ryu* school, becoming *Hanshi* in *Meiji* 36, 9 May 1903. He was a viscount and *Dai Nihon Butokukai* officer, and was head of the *Butokukai-Kenjustu-Kata* enactment.

Unpachiro Shibae b. April 1834, d. 29 October 1912

From the *Shinto munen-Ryu* school and he gained *Hanshi* status on 8 May 1903. He was a committee member for the *Butokukai-Kenjustu-Kata* enactment as well as for the *Dai Nihon Teikoku Kendo Kata* enactment. He was also a police trainer in the *Osaka* and *Oita* prefectures.

Shingoro Negishi b. January 1844 d. 15 September 1913

From the *Shinto munen-Ryu* school and became *Hanshi* on 26 March 1906. He was the teacher for the Imperial Guards *Kendo* school as well as *Butokukai Kenjutsu Kata* enactment committee member. For the *Dai Nihon Teikoku Kendo Kata* enactment he was chairman of the investigation committee.

Shinpei Tsuji b. 15 August 1849 d. 27 July 1914

From the *Shingyoto-Ryu* and *Jikishinkage Ryu* schools, he became *Hanshi* on 5 June 1909. The chairman of the *Dai Nihon Teikoku Kendo Kata* enactment investigation committee, he was also a police trainer in the *Saga* prefecture and was the branch teacher for the *Butokukai* in that *Saga* prefecture.

Tadashi Monna b. April 1855 d. 22 September 1930

From the *Hokkushin Itto Ryu* school he became *Hanshi* on 28 April 1913, and was the chairman for the *Dai Nihon Teikoku Kendo Kata* enactment investigation committee as well as being a committee member when amending the same *Kata* in 1917. He was the professor of the *Bujutsu Senmon Gakko*.

Sasaburo Takano b. June 1862 d. December 1950

From the *Ono Ha Itto Ryu* he became *Hanshi* in April 1913, and was on the committees regarding the *Dai Nihon Teikoku Kendo Kata* enactment, amendment and supplement. He was the Metropolitan Police Officer *Kendo* teacher, and was professor of the Tokyo *Koto Shihan Gakko*.

Takaharu Naito b. 25 October 1862 d. 9 April 1929

From the *Hokushin Itto Ryu*, he was *Hanshi* on 28 April 1913. He had a place on the committees regarding the *Dai Nihon Teikoku Kendo Kata* enactment and amendment, was the Police *Kendo* teacher and professor of *Bujutsu Senmon Gakko*.

Hakudo Nakayama b. February 1873 d. 14 December 1958

From the *Shinto munen Ryu* he became *Hanshi* in May 1920 and was on the committees for the enactment and amendment for the *Dai Nihon Teikoku Kendo Kata* in 1917 and 1933.

Kinnosuke Ogawa b. May 1884 d. 30 March 1962

He was from the *Hokkushin Itto Ryu* school and reached *Hanshi* in May 1927 and the 10th *Dan* after 1957. He was on the committee for the *Dai Nihon Teikoku Kendo Kata* in 1933, and was Professor of *Bujutsu Senmon Gakko*, Lecturer of the *Hiroshima Koto Shihan Gakko* and Police trainer in Aichi.

Moriji Mochida b. January 1885 d. February 1974

From the *Hokkushin Itto Ryu* school be became *Hanshi* in May 1927 and reached 10th *Dan* level after 1957. On the committee for the *Dai Nihon Teikoku Kendo Kata* in 1933, he was a graduate of the *Bujutsu* Teachers Training School and assistant Professor of the *Bujutsu Senmon Gakko*. His teaching continued at the *Butokukai Chiha* prefecture, the *Tokyo Koto Shihan Gakko* and as the police trainer in Korea. He was the champion of *Tenran Shiai* in 1929 when performing in front of the Emperor.

Sosuke Nakano b. September 1885 d. 2 March 1973

He became *Hanshi* in May 1927 and graduated to 10th *Dan* in 1957. He was a graduate of the *Bujutsu* Teacher Training school and later became asistant professor of the same school.

Goro Saimura b. May 1887 d. 13 March 1969

He was *Hanshi* in May 1928 and became 10th *Dan* in 1957. On the committee for the *Dai Nihon Teikoku Kendo Kata* in 1933, he was a graduate of the *Bujutsu* Teacher Training school, the teacher for the Metropolitan Police, the Imperial Guards *kendo* teacher as well as teaching at the Waseda University.

Yuji Oasa b. January 1887 d. 22 February 1974

Although details are scarce it is known that he became *Hanshi* in May 1936 and reached 10th *Dan* in 1957.

THE BREAKDOWN OF TECHNIQUE

By noting the number and type of cut and strike area performed within the *Kata*, we can perhaps draw some conclusions into their relative importance in combative preference.

Totals included are for both attack and defence, and are for both *Tachi* and *Kodachi*.

	Men	**13**
	Kote	**4**
	Tsuki	**4**
	Do	**2**
Oji Waza		
	Nuke	**3**
	Suriage	**3**
	Maki Kaeshi	**1**
	Suri Otoshi	**1**
	Tsuri Nagashi	**1**
	Kiri Musubi	**1**
	Ai-Tsuki	**1**
	Ai-Uchi	**1**
	Uke Nagasu	**2**
	Surikomi	**1**

Kamae positions, after the commencement positions of *chudan kamae* and the following exclude *Kodachi Kamae* as these are classified as covering *Kamae*.

  Also excluded are mid Kata Kamae used for *Sanshin* and through positions

Chudan (inc *Seigan*)	**7**
Jodan	**4**
Gedan	**4**
Hasso	**1**
Waki	**1**

Note that all *kata* begin and end from the *chudan kamae* position.

椿ともいふ、木、火、土、金、水の木に相當し、劔を立木の如く立つるので、心も大木の立てるが如く、泰然自若として敵の動作を監視し、敵の暴動に應じて如何様にも變化し得る構である。

脇構。劔を左脇にとり、劔尖を後方にして斜下に向け、左手を臍の邊に置き、左足を前に踏出して構へる。打を發するには大冠りに打込む。或は揚裂袈胴に打込む。此の構は陰八相の構と同じ心持にて、敵の暴動を監視するを旨とし、必要に應じ取出して用ふるが如く必要に應じて何業にも變化し、自由自在に活動し得られる構である。

中段の構へ（正眼）

刀の持ち方。右手は鍔に密着させ、鍔下約五分位離して握り、左手は柄頭が半ば小指にかかるやう、丁度蝙蝠を握るが如き心持にて軽く取り、又この手状を絞るやうに兩手頸を柄と内に絞り込み、兩胸に力を入れず、打つ時には、拇指と無名指と小指とに力を入れ、左右の手で物を絞り氣味に打つのである。

劔尖の活動。劔尖の活動に重要なもので、敵を攻むるにも、押へるにも、捧くにも、この劔尖の活用によるものである。劔尖には常に精粹を痛め、敵を攻め附け、押へ附ける様な威力を痛へつ、恰も鶺鴒の尾の撞に上下に動かし、迅速に撃入む準備をなし、吾が動作の起りを敵に知らしめざる様にする。敵を攻むる時は劔尖を

— 94 —

Sasaburo Takano as a young man in *Seigan Kamae*

GLOSSARY

A The breath sound of attack (POSITIVE)

Ai jodan Both in high level attitude (*kamae*)

Ai gedan Both in low level attitude (*kamae*)

Ai seigan Both in middle level attitude (*kamae*)

Aitsuki Simultaneous thrust

Aiuchi Simultaneous *Ippon* on each other—both make valid strikes

Ansei Period of Japanese history 1854–59

Asayama Ryu A classical school of swordsmanship

Ashi sabaki Foot movements

Ashi Feet

Ayumi ashi Normal walking

Bokken Wooden sword

Budo Martial ways (SOMETIMES DEFINED AS FOR SELF PERFECTION)

Budoka Practitioner of *budo*

Bujutsu Martial arts (SOMETIMES DEFINED AS FOR SELF PROTECTION)

Bujutsu Kyoin Yoseijo Martial arts masters training school

Bunkyo Period of Japanese history 1861–63

Chi Earth, ground

Chisai Small

Chudan Middle level

Chudan hanmi Position of chudan with *kodachi* against opponent's *Jodan* or *Gedan Kamaes.*

Dai 1, 2, 3 etc *Hon* First, second, third in *Kata*

Dai Nihon Butokukai Former controlling body for *Budoka* founded in 1895

Dan Grade or rank

Do Protective chest armor, call for chest cut (*shinai kendo*)

Dojo Training hall

Ei One of the traditional *kiai* sounds

Enzan no metsuke Looking at a far mountain—way of observing the whole of something

Fumikomi ashi Stamping footwork

Gedan Low level

Gedan ni taisuru How to respond to *gedan* (*kamae* WITH A *kodachi*)

Genji Period of Japanese history 1864, for one year

Go Five

Go burei 'Please pardon me' for being arrogant—*kendo* term expressed when adopting *jodan kamae,* or when non-protected part is struck, or when a good attack is spoiled.

Gohonme 5th long sword form

Go gyo Five streams or five currents as reference to five *kamae* attitudes.

Go gyo no kata *Kata* devised by *Sasaboro Takano* from *Ono Ha Itto Ryu*

Go no sen Counter response to opponent when attacking

Gyo Stream

Hakama Traditional Japanese skirt divided like trousers

Hanmi Half turned attitude of the body

Hanshi Highest teaching title, but only since 1957. The grading system pre 1957 was 1st to 5th *Dan* only, then teaching grade of *Renshi, Kyoshi* and *Hanshi* were awarded

Hara Abdomen or lower stomach area

Hasso *Kamae* of *In* (*Yohonme*).

Hidari Left

Hiki waza Stepping back technique

Hiraki ashi Sideways step

Hito All men

Hitoemi Completely turned body

Hokushin Itto Ryu A classical school of swordsmanship

Iai Sword drawing movement incorporating cut and thrust. Can be *Iai do* or *Iai jutsu*

Ichiden Ryu A classical school of swordsmanship

In Negative *kamae* attitude (*hasso*)

Ippon Referred to as the first point scored

Ippon me First long sword form

Ire zuki ni nagasu Turning attitude of *Hanmi,* so protecting your body by presenting a smaller area (WHEN RECEIVING *tsuki* IN *sanbonme*)

Irimi The action to step into opponent's *Maai* (DRAWING ONE'S LEFT SHOULDER BACK) from *Hanmi* to *Hitoemi* (COMPLETELY TURNED BODY)

Irimi no seme Entering by attacking the body of your opponent

Issoku itto no ma Middle sword distance, tips just crossing (CUT FROM ONE STEP DISTANCE)

Itto Ryu A classical school of swordsmanship

Iya-toh One of the traditional *kiai* sounds

Jigen Ryu A classical school of swordsmanship

Jikishin Kage Ryu A classical school of swordsmanship

Jin Man (ALT. NAME)

Jodan High level when fist is placed higher than the shoulder with a sword

Judo Gentle way, sport of grappling derived from *Jujutsu*

Jujutsu Martial art of locks, strikes and throws, a skill of the *Samurai*

Kaei Period of Japanese history 1848–1853

Kakari Geiko All out attack practice, used in *shinai kendo*

Kakegoe Shout (*kiai*), yell

Kamae Attitude of the body (READY POSITION)

Kamae o toku Position of sword point to your opponent's knee height, blade turned, edge facing left. (BREAKING KAMAE). Relaxing from the ready position

Kamiza High place in the *dojo* (HIGH AS IN RESPECTFUL)

Kao Period of Japanese history 1865–1867
Kata Pre-determined form
Katana Japanese long sword
Keiko Practice
Keiko gi Practice jacket
Keishichoryu Old style police *kata*
Ken saki or **Ken sen** Sword point
Kendo Sword way (SPORT OF JAPANESE FENCING)
Kendoka *Kendo* player
Kenjutsu Killing art, with sword
Ki Spirit, mental energy
Ki Wood or a tree(s)
Kiai Shout (*kakegoe*)
Kiaitari Threatening a thrust to your opponent
Kigurai Noble bearing, proud in attitude
Kin Gold
Kiri musubi Simultaneous cutting and locking together of swords
Kobushi Fist
Kodachi Short sword (WOOD OR METAL)
Koka Period of Japanese history 1844–1847
Komainu Lion/dog-like statue, temple guardian seen outside Shinto shrines
Kote Glove protectors used in *shinai kendo*
Koto Shihan Gakko Teachers training college, forerunner of
        Tsukuba University, Tokyo
Kumitachi Alternative name for *kata*
Kurai seme Feeling of walking forward, intent on an unstoppable thrust
Kurama Ryu A classical school of swordsmanship
Kusa Weeds, grass
Kyoshi 2nd highest teaching title
Kyoto Old capital city of Japan, before Tokyo (*Edo*)
Ma or **Maai** Distance
Maki kaeshi Turning deflection
Mawari geiko Rotating practice procedure
Meiji Period of Japanese history 1868–1911
Men Protective head wear (FACE MASK & HELMET COMBINED); call for
        attacking head cut
Migi Right
Mizu Water
Montsuki Kimono with family crest (*mon*) printed on the back and sleeves
Mu Gamae Open attitude (NO POSITION)
Nanahonme 7th long sword form (*kata*)
Nihon Japan (ALT. NAME) (Also the second, No. 2)
Nihonme 2nd long sword form (*kata*)
Nin Man
No Of
Nodo Throat
Nuki Evasion
Okuri ashi Foot movement by slide step, maintaining the leading foot forward
Ono Ha Itto Ryu A classical school of swordsmanship
Osame to Sheath sword, put it away

O tagai ni rei Mutual bow to your partner (OPPONENT)

Rei Bow

Renshi First teaching title

Rishin Ryu A classical school of swordsmanship

Ropponme 6th long sword form (*kata*)

Ryu School

Ryuha A branch or section of that school

Saga Prefecture in *Kyushu* (SOUTH ISLAND OF JAPAN)

Sage to or **Tei to** Arm held by your side, gripping sword in sheathed-like position. (*Tei* means "to hang")

Sageo The tying cord of the *katana*

Samurai Warrior class of Japan

Sanbonme 3rd long sword form (*kata*)

Seigan Alternative older name for *chudan* (CLEAR EYES)

Seigan ni taisuru In response to *Seigan* (*chudan*) *no kamae* (*kodachi*)

Seiho Alt. old name for *kata*

Seiza Kneeling down position

Sen Forestall, take the initiative to have victory

Sen Sen, No Sen Anticipate your opponent's intention

Sensei Teacher

Seme Pushing forward, looking to break your opponent's guard

Shidachi The part of the winner taken in *kata* (THE STUDENT)

Shin Truth

Shinai Bamboo practice sword used in *kendo*

Shinai Kendo Fencing in protective *kendo* armor using bamboo swords

Shinken Shobu Contest to the outcome of one survivor often to the death

Shinogi Raised edge on the side of a sword or *bokken*

Shinto Original Animistic religion of Japan

Shinto Munen Ryu A classical school of swordsmanship

Shizentai Normal standing position

Shogun Military ruler or dictator, the true ruling power in Japan until the *Meiji* restoration (RETURN TO FULL POWER OF THE EMPEROR)

Shomen Front directed cut to the head area

Showa Period of Japanese history 1926–1989

Showa Ten Ran Shiai Competition performed in front of the Emperor

So Weeds, grass (*kusa*)

Sonkyo Crouch-like stance for starting and finishing in *Shinai Kendo* and *kata*

Suki Opening for attacks

Suriage Deflection technique

Surinagasu Technique of cutting down the blade of your opponent with a horizontal action (AS SEEN IN 3RD *kodachi* FORM)

Suri ashi Glide walk

Tachi Long sword (WOOD OR METAL) alt. name

Taisho Period of Japanese history 1912–1925

Taito Sword held at waist height (*Tai* MEANS A BELT)

Tare Protective apron, part of armor used in *Shinai Kendo*

Teikoku Imperial

Ten Heaven

Tenpo Period of Japanese history 1830

Toh *Kiai* sound used in *kata* (BREATH OF DEFENSE)

Tokugawa Family name of *shogun* (THAT RULED JAPAN FROM 1603–1869)

Tsuka   Handle or hilt of sword, *shinai* or *bokken*

Tsuki   Thrust

Tsuba   Protective hand guard on sword, *shinai* or *bokken*

Uchidachi   Part taken as loser in *kata* (THE TEACHER)

Uke Nagasu (Nagashi)   *Kodachi* technique, let the opponent's attacking sword slide down along one's blade

Un   Breath sounds of defense (NEGATIVE)

Ura   Inside (reverse)

Waki gamae   Attitude of sword concealed behind your back (*yo*) (POSITIVE)

Waza   Technique

Yagyu Ryu   A classical school of swordsmanship

Yah   *Kiai* sounds used in *kata* (BREATH OF ATTACK USED BY *Uchidachi*)

Yah-eh   One of the original *kiai* sounds

Yang   Positive (CHINESE) equ. to *YO*

Yin   Negative (CHINESE) equ. to *IN*

Yo   *Waki Gamae* (POSITIVE)

Yohonme   4th long sword form (*kata*)

Yondan   4th rank (DEGREE), grade of

Zanshin   Awareness, unbroken concentration after an attack is finished

Zen Nihon Kendo Renmei   Governing body of *kendo* in Japan